PHILosophically Speaking

The stories and musings of an Appalachian preacher, teacher, and psychologist

By Phil LeMaster

Copyright © 2009 by Phil LeMaster

PHILosophically Speaking
by Phil LeMaster

Printed in the United States of America

ISBN 9781615794072

All rights reserved solely by the author. The author guarantees all contents are original and do not infringe upon the legal rights of any other person or work. No part of this book may be reproduced in any form without the permission of the author. The views expressed in this book are not necessarily those of the publisher.

Unless otherwise indicated, Bible quotations are taken from The Holy Bible, New International Version, Grand Rapids. Copyright © 1978 by Zondervan Bible Publishers.

www.xulonpress.com

Mr. and Mrs. Dunn,

Thanks for being such a blessing! Hope you enjoy this look back at our ministry and life.

In Christ!, Love,

Phil

DEDICATION

To my loving wife, Teresa; our two wonderful daughters, Mandi and Megan; my amazing son-in-law, Chris; and the two most precocious grandchildren in the world, Maizy and Kai!

ACKNOWLEDGEMENTS

I want to express my appreciation to the leadership of the Franklin Christian Church for granting me sabbatical time to complete this project: Bob Bell, John Clark, Doug Fultz, Jack Holloway, Steve Marshall, David Pinson, Steve Shelton, and Greg Turner.

I am thankful for the patient efforts of the two church secretaries who edited most of my articles through the years and saw that they met weekly deadlines: the late Cheryl Hamm Ball of Central Christian Church, Ironton, Ohio, and Vicki Gilbert, First Church of Christ, Grayson, Kentucky. I also want to thank Randy Brown for his meticulous proofing of the initial manuscript.

Most of all I am grateful to my loving Heavenly Father who sent his Son, Jesus Christ, into this world to redeem me from my sins and to allow the Holy Spirit to dwell within me.

TABLE OF CONTENTS

Introduction xv

Part I — Family 19

  1. An Answered Prayer 23

  2. Mine! 28

  3. Scoot Back, Daddy, Scoot Back 31

  4. The Sound of Music 34

  5. Motivated Behavior 38

  6. Speak Their Language 42

  7. How Not to Parent 45

  8. Beauty Is in the Eye of the Beholder 49

  9. Ode to the Empty Nest 52

10. God's Shovel	55
11. God and Chocolate	60
12. Tasteless Sin	63
13. Over the Rainbow	66
14. It Hurts So Good	69
15. It's a Boy!	72
16. My Son Is Drunk?	76

Part II — Things 79

1. Combs	81
2. Permanent	84
3. What Time Is It?	87
4. Platinum	90
5. Green Side Up!	93
6. Shattered Dreams	96
7. Ladybugs	99
8. Lowell's Syndrome	102
9. Tee's A-Plenty	105
10. Tommy	108

11. Vanity Plates 111

12. Raw Umber and Burnt Sienna 114

Part III—School 119

1. The Fear Factor 123

2. Life Lesson from a Cheese Cube 127

3. Stay in the Game 130

4. My First Flashbulb Memory 133

5. A Lesson in Humility 136

6. My Tobacco Role 139

7. Help from an Atheist 143

8. He Is the Boss of Me! 146

Part IV—Home 151

1. Dying Where You Live 155

2. The Best Template 158

3. My Clothes! 161

4. My Favorite Meal 164

5. Blackberries 167

6. It Pays to Follow Instructions 170

7. Grandma's Pickled Corn 173

8. The Disappearing Whipped Cream 176

9. The American Patriot 179

10. My Mother's Hands 183

11. Solanum Tuberosum 186

12. Haircut Day 189

13. My Cousin's Tears 192

14. Yellow Bird 197

Part V — Experiences 201

1. A Small Change Can Make a Big Difference 203

2. Tiger's Muff 206

3. Amazing Grace 209

4. Reflections of an Old Man 213

5. School Daze 217

6. Superman Is Dead 220

7. Shaking Trees 223

8. Trophies in the Attic 226

9. Heavenly Real Estate 229
10. The Real Proof of the Unisex Fallacy 232
11. What's on My Silver Shelf? 235
12. A Job Worth Doing 238
13. A Ton or an Ounce 241
14. Loser's Limp 244

Part VI — Church 247

1. Mt. Olivet 249
2. Let Me Have Christmas 252
3. Leaving Jesus Out 255
4. Eternity 258
5. A Summer Silent Night 261
6. The Rich Little Boys of Mozambique 264
7. No Coincidences 267
8. Helping Your Neighbor 270
9. Casting a Vote against a Familiar Foe 273
10. Something Happened Here 276
11. One Mistake 279

12. Dr. Strangeglove 282

13. Prospects, Suspects and Others................................285

14. Check!...289

15. The Danger of Isolation 292

16. DiMaggio and the Umpire 295

17. Send Up Lumber..298

18. A President's Bible 301

19. Life in a Jar 304

Part VII—People..**307**

1. The Influence of a Life and a Death...........................309

2. Pursued by the Hound of Heaven 312

3. Life Begins at Eighty 315

4. A Heart that Is Finally Whole 318

5. A Question from Stephanie 321

6. The Cost of Following Jesus......................................324

7. Misadventures in the Smithsonian 327

8. Like Father, Like Son...330

9. On Any Street Anywhere 333

INTRODUCTION

With the advent of the Internet and websites for local churches, the hard-copy church newsletter is quickly becoming a thing of the past. This paper organ that seemed such a good idea when I became a minister four decades ago is being replaced by the e-letter, online blogs, Twitter, and who knows what is next! Please understand that this is not the lament of an old guy who is resisting change, but an old guy who understands that outdated methods must give way to newer, better ideas.

The church newsletter, however, was a great way to communicate weekly with the entire congregation back in the days when many of us preachers in small to mid-size churches especially needed such a vehicle. Admittedly, in those early days of ministry, I spent more time in the church office than I wanted to and felt that if you pricked my skin mimeograph ink would probably run out! Yet looking back, I believe that the church newsletter enhanced my work as a minister in every congregation I served.

Beginning with *The Mt. Olivet Christian* in our first ministry in 1970, I edited such a church publication through the completion of our ministry at Grayson, Kentucky, in 2006. I began writing a personal column for these publications somewhere along the way and eventually the column took on the name *PHILosophically Speaking.*

This column furnished me a means of helping congregations to understand who their preacher was and what he believed in a very personal way. It allowed me to open the windows of the parsonage, at my discretion, so that our church family could see and understand my family. It provided me also with a forum for discussing issues, doctrinal and otherwise, that were in my head and on my heart.

To be honest, this column seldom contained heady, philosophical issues. Rather, with a folksy style and a touch of whimsy, I used the column to reinforce common truths and to comment conservatively on issues facing our community, our nation and our world. Some of these articles would circulate more widely, ending up in the local newspaper, church brotherhood journals, or online sermon illustration services.

On a number occasions throughout the years, parishioners and others suggested that I needed to compile a book utilizing the best of these articles. This effort represents my attempt to comply.

It should be noted that this work is somewhat autobiographical in nature because the stories, all true, are my stories. My life journey has been such a blessed one because of the goodness of my Heavenly Father. It has, however, not always been an easy journey due to the makeup of my personality and my failure sometimes to follow God's leading. If I have failed to display all of my warts in these pieces, it is probably because I tend to hide them just like everybody else. I can assure you that they do exist, but are superseded in my life by the wonderful grace of my Lord.

You may also notice that there is a basic chronological arrangement to most of the chapters or sections in this book. This arrangement helped me to provide a workable outline for the material that covers not only four decades of ministry, but also six decades of life. Although most of the articles were easy to categorize, some were not such an easy fit. If you find an article that seems to be in the wrong chapter, you are probably right!

I hope that this little volume in the end conveys the message that my journey in Christ has been a wonderful one. In spite of my personal stumbles, I have found God to be faithful to all of His promises. His word is true and He can be trusted. Praise His name!

PART I—FAMILY

The nuclear family is defined as "a family group that consists only of father, mother, and children."[1] In our fragmented world of the twenty-first century, to be blessed with a nuclear family that is intact and fully functioning is one of the greatest gifts that the individual can have. I am fortunate to be so blessed.

Not only have my wife, Teresa, and I been happily married for almost four decades, both of us were reared in homes where divorce and separation were foreign concepts. Her parents were married for over sixty years before her mother, Gladys, went home to be with the Lord. My parents were married for over forty years when death abruptly took my father from this life to glory. My mother lived as a widow for over thirty years, missing the love of her life until her dying day at the age of ninety-four.

Because the intact nuclear family is so rare in 2009, our troubled world reflexively seems to be lauding the brokenness of the home. The media portrayal is one in which the Beaver Cleaver model of the 1950s is lampooned and lambasted. If you watch much television, go to many movies, or listen to the radio, then you know what I am saying is true. Any media presentation of a home where a man is still married to his first wife and they have children is a picture of laughable proportions *ala Archie Bunker* or worse.

I simply share these stories about our immediate family to say that it is possible to follow the biblical model of one man and one woman in a committed relationship with children who are both blessed and a blessing. And then there are grandchildren! Acknowledging God's grace upon our home most of all, Teresa and I have worked hard to fulfill the vows we made to God and to each other on that December day back in 1969.

Neither of us makes a claim to having been a perfect mate or perfect parents. But we have trusted God and tried our best and He has kept His promises—and more. If these stories are skewed more towards the positive side, please understand there are other stories that I could tell, but won't!

1.

An Answered Prayer

I was finishing up my second year at Kentucky Christian College, strongly exploring the possibility of becoming a preacher. My best friend, Howard "Howdy" Hill, a fellow sophomore, was also considering God's call upon his life.

Between classes, playing basketball for the college, working at The Commercial Bank of Grayson on Saturdays, and preaching at the Carter Christian Church on Sundays; my schedule was full. There was very little time for socializing or dating. It was certainly not that I was disinterested in the opposite sex; there just wasn't room for girls on my calendar.

Howdy, ever the practical one, approached me near the end of the school year with the pressing issue. "Phil," he said, "you know that no churches will call us to be their preachers unless we are married."

Of course, what he was saying was true. No congregation really wants a single, unattached pastor. The problems in hiring a young preacher who is unmarried are simply too many for a congregation of any size to even consider. The stability of having a wife was an unwritten and unspoken necessity for a full-time preaching position.

Howdy continued, "We both need to find a wife before we graduate."

A few days later we finished our spring semester, but Howdy's suggestion—or warning—continued to play on my mind. So I decided to start praying fervently that God would send the right young lady into my life as a help mate. It is this prayer that would become the first entry in *My Catalog of Answered Prayers*, an important mental list in my spiritual heart that I call upon especially when I am discouraged.

The fall semester arrived and Howdy and I were back for our junior years. The first day on campus we saw two very attractive students, both members of the new freshmen class. As we went to dinner in the college cafeteria that same Sunday afternoon, Howdy quizzed me about my potential interest in one of the two girls.

What can I say? The best way I can describe her is that long before Bo Derek and her famous movie role, this girl was a "10." With long blonde hair and striking features, she was simply the most beautiful young lady I have ever seen! Howdy fortunately was attracted to the other girl, a pretty brunette.

"Do you want to ask them out?" Howdy questioned. Of course, I answer with a "yes," not realizing that he meant right then.

No sooner had I given him my response, the two girls walked out of the cafeteria. Howdy literally grabbed me by the arm and walked over to them and said, "Hi, I am Howdy Hill and this is Phil LeMaster. He is preaching tonight at

Carter Christian Church. Would you girls like to go with us to the service?"

I doubt that they were any more surprised at his boldness than I was. The blonde, Teresa Messer, looked at the brunette, Cheryl Edwards, and then she turned to us and said only one word, "No." I am sure that Howdy had some kind of rejoinder, but I was too busy trying to sink into the woodwork to hear!

Amazing as it may sound, less than two years later, Howdy married Cheryl Edwards, and the following week, Teresa Messer and I became husband and wife in a wedding ceremony at the First Christian Church in Olive Hill, Kentucky.

I sometimes still marvel at the way we met, but I marvel even more at God's wonderful answer to my prayer. Teresa and I will soon celebrate our fortieth anniversary, and I consider myself the most blessed husband in the world. My "10" is just as beautiful on the inside as she is on the outside and has been the perfect preacher's wife.

When people question me about answered prayer, I always think of God sending Teresa into my life. I could have searched the world over and never found a more wonderful spouse or partner in ministry. I have learned that if you have a legitimate need in life, ask God with fervent specificity. You may be surprised and delighted at His response!

2.

Mine!

I will never forget the Sunday when our firstborn, Mandi, taught us a lesson about how not to give! She was a toddler at the time and was going into her initial Sunday school class from the nursery. All week long Teresa had been coaching her about the proper etiquette for her new class, including how to put money into the offering plate. She had bought Mandi a little white purse to hold the money to give in her class, and mother and daughter seemed excited about the upcoming new experience.

They rehearsed the routine over and over again. The pretend offering tray was put in front of Mandi and she reached into her "pursie" as she called it and took the coins and placed them in the tray. These practice sessions went well and it was obvious to both of us that Mandi was ready to mimic the appropriate stewardship behavior as she moved up from the nursery to the Toddlers' Class.

Sunday morning came and Mandi was dressed in a new outfit, complete with black patent leather shoes and her new purse. Teresa placed some coins in her purse. It was Dad's turn to rehearse with her one final time before Sunday school.

"You're going to Sunday school class this morning, aren't you?" I asked. She nodded her head and said, "Yes."

"And you're going to give your money to Jesus, aren't you?" I continued. She looked up at me and said, "No!" And then, clutching her little white purse to her chest, she added, "It's mine. It's mine."

How quickly in life we learn to claim ownership of the things God gives us to use as His stewards. Teresa and I were disheartened to see our little girl react in such a selfish way, but we shouldn't have been surprised. Mandi was barely two, but she already understood this world's principle about material things: if I have possession of something, then it belongs to me.

Of course, this principle is wrong. Any possession we have in this world belongs to God and is only on loan to us until He needs it or until He calls us home. In time, Mandi would learn this truth and develop a giving spirit. Today she sometimes surprises us with her open hands and open heart in her relationship with God and others.

The point is that she had to learn to give. At two, she was a typical toddler—self-centered and grasping. We all are at that age. Giving is a grace that must be taught to children. Lesson one just didn't work at our house.

FOR THE WORLD

EVERY TRIBE. EVERY TONGUE. EVERY NATION.

26 MISSIONARIES & CHURCH PLANTERS
Barnabas 10/40 - Dwight and Gayle Tomlinson
Ethiopia, Africa - Josh and Ruth Lovegrove
Kenya, Africa - Ron and Christie Enoch
Senegal, Africa - Patrick and Jody Russell
Australia - Bill and Doyla Bramblet
Belgium - Larry and Jean Taylor
Brazil - John and Neila Yelle
Cambodia - Stephen and Angela Benefield
China - John and Cathy Honeycutt
Costa Rica - Ed and Norma Bordell
England - Ryan and Elizabeth Strother
*France - Kyle and Abigail
Indonesia - Philip and Kristine Lien
*Indonesia - Thomas and Kezia Bui
Israel - Dr. Ramzi and Ruth Kammar
Japan - Jimmy and Sarah Pak
Mexico - Luis and Maggie Montaño
Mexico - Dan and Debbie Morris
Murrieta, CA - Dominic and Amanda Kalmeta
Cebu City, Philippines - David and Angel Cabuntala
Spain - Justin and Grace Hayes
Spain - Josep and Sara Segurado
*Tempe, AZ - Jon and Amy Guy
Thailand - Brian and Jamie Cone
US Military Overseas - Jeffery and Andrea Wright
Vanuatu - Jeremy and Elizabeth Pinero

4 MINISTRIES SUPPORTED
Fremont, CA - Compassion Network
*Laguna, Philippines - Bay Area Baptist Church
Lancaster, CA - West Coast Baptist College
Temecula, CA - Mighty Oaks Warrior Programs

3 SPECIAL LOVE OFFERINGS
Barnabas 10/40 - Special Project in India ($3,100)
Tempe, AZ - Citypoint Baptist Church ($2,000)
Laguna, Philippines - Bay Area Baptist Church ($500)

***New for 2019**

2929 PERALTA BLVD
FREMONT CA 94536
510.797.8882
BAY AREA BAPTIST CHURCH

: Pastors :-

1) Dinakaran garu
2) Satish Kumar garu
3) Samuel Karmoji garu
4) Stephen paul - Shailapaul garu
5) Johnwesly garu
6) Ajayanna g
7) Kiran garu
8) Moshe pastor garu
9) Johnwelt pastor garu
10) Daniel garu (Singer)
11) Bay area Baptist church Morris pastor

46 Slots

Divya → neet exam
levi → Neet " score
prasy → sat exam dec 1st week

Ajayanna
Moses bro
Kiran pastor
Sravanthi akka
Shama
Rohini
aswini
priya akka
sandeepa
Jeff pastor

3.

Scoot Back, Daddy, Scoot Back

I had accepted the call as senior minister of the Central Christian Church in Ironton, Ohio, a large congregation with over one thousand resident members. This vibrant church had recently erected a huge state-of-the-art building, resulting in a major indebtedness. Feeling the pressure of my new responsibilities and with a strong desire to impress my parishioners, I had hit the ground running. I was in the office early every day and almost every evening found me out shepherding the flock or reaching out to potential church members.

My wife, Teresa, was very understanding, but our little daughter, Mandi, at two and one-half years of age was perplexed by my absence from home. She loved for me to read to her after dinner each evening and it was a practice that I continued in my new position—with one caveat. I would sit on the edge of my recliner with her seated by my side and read a quick story or two before rushing out for another night of harried activity.

One evening Mandi said something that jolted me back to reality about my role as a father. I had sat down with her in my recliner, once again on the edge, ready to quickly read and run. Mandi stopped me and, patting the recliner seat, said, "Scoot back, Daddy, scoot back." She knew on those rare occasions when I wasn't going out for the evening that I would relax, sit back in my recliner, and leisurely read stories to her heart's content.

Her words pierced my soul as I understood what she was really saying, "Slow down, Daddy, please. Make time for me." Appropriately chastened, I scooted back.

This is a lesson that busy fathers everywhere need to take to heart. Sometimes in our mad rush to make a living for ourselves and our families, we forget to make a life. We spend our time trying to impress the wrong people with the wrong motives and are guilty of making the poorest impression in the one place where it really matters—on the home front.

4.

The Sound of Music

The big day had finally arrived and our Mandi was excited, but sick. She had awakened with a temperature of almost 102°F and was obviously coming down with something. With such a determined little girl on our hands, we knew a family crisis was brewing.

For weeks Mandi had been practicing with Teresa in preparation for auditioning for the local high school's spring production, *The Sound of Music*. Our song bird, Mandi, had an amazing voice, even then as a six-year old. Her mother had told her about the audition and suggested that perhaps Mandi could play the part of Gretl, the youngest of the von Trapp children in the story. The audition required the singing of the song, "Do-Re-Mi," before the play's production team.

The older of our two daughters, Mandi has always had a big sister's mentality and a determination of steel. As sick as she was, she was not interested in hearing her mother tell her that the 4 p.m. audition was off. From the safe distance of the church office, I monitored the situation as mother and daughter battled it out concerning the decision. The afternoon came and Mandi's temperature was not going down.

To say that my wife was and is a wonderful mother is an understatement. Like a protective hen she hovered over our two girls in their growing up years, especially when it came to matters of physical health. Mandi was too sick to audition and that was it, period. Or perhaps I should say question mark! By 3 p.m. Mandi's tears and persuasive words had prevailed, and I was summons home to take her to the audition while Teresa stayed with Megan, our one-year old.

We arrived at the music room at Ironton High School with time to spare. The room filled quickly with chattering children and nervous parents. Given Mandi's condition, it was fortunate that Gretl was the first audition role. Mandi was, by far, the youngest child trying for the role and so they let her go first. For some reason, she didn't want dad in the room while she sang, and so I went out into the hall and leaned against the door to listen.

With an amazingly clear voice in spite of her illness, Mandi sang out the words, "Doe-a deer, a female deer; Ray-a drop of golden sun…" Not missing a word or a note, our little girl finished up strong, "Do re mi fa so la te do." The applause in the audition room that followed seemed much more than perfunctory, at least to this very biased eavesdropper.

Her task done, Mandi was free to go. The auditions would continue, and a couple of days later we would receive the verdict. The part would go to a diminutive third-grader who could read and would be able to stay for the late rehearsals. Mandi was momentarily disappointed, but undeterred. She was establishing a habit that continues to serve her well in life, the habit of finishing what she starts with great determination.

Some parents would disagree with our decision to let Mandi audition, given the circumstances. I cannot disagree with your disagreement! But if we had it to do all over again, I know our decision would be the same. Our songbird had launched her career in the most unlikely fashion, and God continues to use her voice to bless countless others today.

5.

Motivated Behavior

At the outset, I thought it was one of those genius parenting ideas that needed to be sent to *Focus on the Family* for wider distribution. In retrospect, I am not so sure. We were living in Ironton at the time and had a beautiful ornamental crabapple tree in our backyard. Simply glorious in the spring, the flowering pink petals of the tree canopied about one-third of our lawn behind our house.

Of course, this tree was just as prodigious in producing its fruit as it was in the blossoming process. For the uninitiated, ornamental is the key to the description of this particular variety of the crabapple. Ornamental as in look at it, but don't waste your time trying to eat it! The tiny marble-size apples were not considered poisonous, just worthless as a food crop.

Come late July the tiny crabapples began to fall from the tree by the thousands. Now, unless you've ever had a healthy flowering crabapple, you think that I am exaggerating. I am not! The resultant debris carpeted the same square footage as the previous blossoms had canopied, making it almost impossible to mow the backyard with any degree of success.

Oh, I tried mowing, but rolling over the fallen apples produced a very uneven pattern that was simply unacceptable. Rake them? Have you ever tried to rake up 300 square feet of ornamental crabapples, sometimes stacked two or three high? There had to be a better way!

And using my great psychological acumen, I found it. "Give the girls sufficient motivation for the job and turn them loose," I thought to myself.

The next morning before I went to the church office, I gave them the challenge, "If you will help Dad by picking up the crabapples in the backyard, I will pay you $1 for every pound."

As I drove home from church that evening, I was still congratulating myself on how smart I was. I envisioned the crabapples gone; my backyard ready for a *Home and Gardens'* photo shoot, and a cost of about $15. Given a preacher's salary, that was a pretty steep price, but I was willing to pay it to be rid of the problem.

Excitedly, Mandi and Megan greeted me at the front door. They hurried me outside to the backyard to show me their work. On our patio was shopping bag after shopping bag filled to the brim with crabapples! To the tune of $35 worth! When I weighed them, Mandi had picked twenty-six pounds and Megan nine pounds of the marble-size problems.

Yes, the grass under and around the tree was completely cleared of the mess, but at a much higher price than I had planned to pay. Believing in immediate reinforcement, I am sure I had to make a quick trip to the ATM to withdraw the necessary funds.

I would later learn that the girls had finished the job quickly and Mandi had then pulled hundreds of crabapples off of the low-lying branches to increase her production. Smart girl, really…much more so than her Dad!

6.

Speak Their Language

The North American Christian Convention was being held in Indianapolis that particular summer in conjunction with the National Missionary Convention. Because the two groups were meeting together, there were several thousand more people present than for our normal annual gathering.

Being a family convention, the NACC always provides programming for children and youth. Due to the swelled attendance, all programs were filled to overflowing and the children's activities were almost zoo-like in their frenzy.

Our younger daughter, Megan, was seven at the time. We left her one evening at the children's program so we could attend the worship service at the adjacent Hoosier Dome. The staffers placed a purple badge with a number on Megan's shirt and gave the corresponding numbered purple badge to my wife, Teresa. In those days before pagers and video ID, it was a good method for assuring that the children would end up with the right parents at the end of day.

Following the worship service, Teresa and I stopped by the exhibit area to visit with friends. Suddenly realizing that Megan was missing, Teresa dispatched me to the children's programming area to pick her up. It was only after I arrive at the site that I happened to remember that Teresa had the matching purple badge tucked away in her purse.

It was a quarter-mile walk back to the exhibit area, so I explained the reason for my missing badge to the childcare workers and asked them to let me take Megan anyway. I could see the reluctance in their eyes. Turning to Megan,

I said, "You'll verify that I am your Daddy, won't you, Meggy?"

She looked up at me with a puzzled look on her face and then turned to the workers and said, "No."

Our older daughter, Mandi, was with me and together it took the two of us about ten more minutes to convince the workers that a kid that looked so much like her father had to be my daughter. Finally, they were willing to release her into our custody!

Outside in the hall, I expressed my aggravation with Megan, "Megan, why did you say 'no'?"

With hurt and equal aggravation in her voice, she replied, "Daddy, I didn't know what that big word 'verify' meant."

Of course she didn't. It was a good reminder to me that when you are talking with kids, especially your own, you better speak their language!

7.

How Not to Parent

One of my favorite topics to address, either from the pulpit or in the classroom, is the subject of discipline and children. As a psychologist as well as a minister, I have a very thorough understanding of the war going on between fundamental Christianity and childhood development specialists on this issue. To say that the two groups are at polar opposites on what constitutes good discipline is probably a fair statement.

My purpose here is not to give my personal primer on the subject, although I will be quick to point out that Teresa and I had a red fly swatter that had a prominent place in our kitchen closet and that this "neutral object" was never used to swat flies!

I generally conclude my strong recommendations about childrearing and discipline by letting people know that this preacher-psychologist and his wife were not always good at the job! I do so by telling them of the time we really blew it with our older daughter, Mandi.

It was after dark on a late fall evening and we were returning as a family from visiting Teresa's folks in Olive Hill, Kentucky. The return trip to Ironton, Ohio, from Olive Hill is about fifty miles. You travel the interstate highway for about thirty-five miles, then exit and take state routes to complete the journey.

Mandi was twelve years old at the time, quickly heading into her adolescent years. Always a strong-willed young lady, she had recently developed a mouth to match her age. (If you don't understand that last sentence, you either have no children or your children have not reached pubescence yet!) She and her mother became involved in a heated conversation about something that increased in intensity as we drove the thirty-five miles on the interstate.

The discussion reached the boiling point just as we exited I-64 onto Route 60 near Summit, KY. Mandi finally half-yelled, "I want out of this car!"

To my utter surprise, my mild-mannered wife retorted, "Okay! Phil, stop the car and let her out!"

It is at this point in the story that I would like to say that with calmness in my voice, I was able to defuse the situation and return our family to our usual state of bliss. I would like to say that, but I can't! Totally fed up myself, I stopped the car alongside Route 60 and told Mandi to get out. And she did! And then we drove off!!

Please understand that it was about 9 p.m., a moonless night, and we are in the middle of nowhere! As you are probably hoping, it only took about one-half mile of travel for sanity to return to the occupants in our car. We made a quick U-turn, retraced our steps and found our daughter sitting on the hillside, hands folded and a frown creasing her face. In spite of her displeasure with her parents, Mandi readily got back in the car and we traveled the last fifteen miles of our trip in almost total silence.

Since I believe that the statute of limitations on such child cruelty has expired, I now feel free to share this story in print for the first time. Truthfully, the lesson to be learned on that night was for Dad and Mom. For a home to function well, there always has to be at least one person acting like an adult. Unfortunately, for about five minutes on that particular night, we were all children.

8.

Beauty Is in the Eye of the Beholder

"What did you think? She looked alright, but did you notice how she almost tripped on that one move?" I leaned over and whispered in Teresa's ear my personal opinion of the particular Miss Kentucky candidate's dance routine. It is amazing how quickly you can become a critic, especially when your daughter happens to be a participant.

And I was not the only one in the audience with an opinion. Of the 250 or so people present, all looked with critical eyes as thirty of the bravest young ladies in the state displayed their talent for public scrutiny.

Teresa and I, of course, looked with jaundiced eyes at twenty-nine of the performers. We noticed every misstep, heard every off-key note, and even found ourselves critiquing the pianists who were playing classical pieces I had only heard as background music in childhood cartoons.

But when Contestant Number 17 stepped to the stage and began singing "On My Own" from *Les Miserables,* we took off our critical glasses and cheered every right note. We stopped looking for flaws and mistakes and applauded every proper phrase. In our book, Megan's performance was perfect.

Interesting, isn't it? How we view others in life depends not so much on their performance as our predisposition towards them. If we like them, they can do little wrong. But if we dislike them, chances are that we will interpret much they do in a negative light. And when they really make a misstep or hit a sour note, we are effusive with our righteous condemnation!

Just for the record, I am glad that God isn't like me. With Jesus Christ as my Lord and Savior, I know that my Heavenly Father looks upon me with eyes of grace and compassion. Oh, don't get me wrong, He is not blind to my mistakes. But He is looking for me to succeed, not fail. As a loving Father, he leans over the golden balcony of heaven and sees my potential, my possibilities. He whispers in my ear and tells me that "all things are possible through Christ" (Philippians 4:13). He believes in me.

And I need to start believing in others. Looking at them with unprejudiced eyes, I need to see beyond their flaws and look for their potential. After all, they are created in the image of God just like me. The God who is changing you and me can change them as well. We believe that, don't we?

9.

Ode to the Empty Nest*

The house is strangely silent,

No music in the walls.

The bathroom's neat and tidy,

No clutter in the halls.

The phone line is unbusy,

The remote control is mine!

The cupboard shelves are full,

Countless choices when we dine.

I stand beside her doorway

And find her bedroom neat.

Her closet is clean and straight,

Once an impossible feat!

Her toy monkey swings from the ceiling,

Her dolls pose on the bed;

Her vanity top is empty

No rouge or lipstick red.

No CD player blaring,

When it's time to take our rest.

Our Meggie's now in college

And ours is an empty nest.

They say the many plusses

Outweigh the minuses here.

"You're free at last!" they tell us,

As we wipe away a tear.

For her we're really happy,

As excited as can be.

For us, we're not so certain

That the empty nest is glee.

Wait! An inspiring thought just hit me

To put an end to my woes

Megan will be home on Friday,

To do her dirty clothes.

*Poem penned when our younger daughter, Megan, left home for nearby Kentucky Christian College.

10.

God's Shovel

It was a hard decision for Teresa and me to make, but one that seemed necessary if the building program at First Church in Grayson, Kentucky, was going to move forward. With a building constructed in 1921 that was no longer adequate for our growing congregation, a new worship complex was desperately needed. The cost of the new structure with the property acquisition was going to be over $1.5 million and require a leap of faith by our group of 250 active members.

Prayerfully, we hired a stewardship counselor and launched into a three-year building fund stewardship campaign. The counselor told me upfront that as senior minister, my family would have to set the example commitment-wise and be transparent about that commitment. I don't know what I was more uncomfortable with at that point, the making of the commitment or the transparency.

But after much discussion and prayer, Teresa and I decided to make a commitment to the stewardship campaign that would require us to double our then current giving level. To be honest, we did not have a clue as to where that extra money would be found. We had the usual expenses of most couples our age with car payments, a house payment, and the sundry other expenses necessitated in the rearing of two daughters. Beyond these financial responsibilities, we had higher education dreams for both Mandi and Megan. The new commitment would mean if they went to college, all of the money would have to be borrowed. Our new budget would have no room for even a partial college fund for our girls.

With the usual slogans used for such giving campaigns, we assured our people that God could be trusted to take care of our needs if we put Him first. We reminded them that we are mere stewards of what He has loaned to us for a time. We own nothing in reality.

"God will be a debtor to no man," I said from the pulpit, believing in my heart of hearts that the statement was true, but wondering in a practical sense how He was going perform such a miracle. Deciding to simply trust Him, we made our first week's gift by faith, knowing that there were 155 similar weeks ahead before the giving campaign was to be completed.

God is faithful. We never missed a week of giving and had the additional blessing of an increased buoyancy of faith because we were leaning on God financially like never before. By the end of the campaign, our older daughter was in college at Belmont University in Nashville, Tennessee, with full tuition, room and board, and even books paid for by a wonderful scholarship. The scholarship even took care of most of her graduate school expenses as well.

When our younger daughter was ready for a college, a special scholarship fund set up for employees' families at Kentucky Christian College paid for our Megan's tuition, room and board. Her only expenses during her four years at the Grayson, Kentucky, college would be textbooks and incidental fees. Their indebtedness and ours for their college expense when both graduated was zero!

Our stewardship campaign would need to be renewed at least twice for three-year periods each time. We would continue our commitments and God would continue to bless beyond measure. I sat down one day and added up the extra money we had given and the amount the two scholarships had covered for our girls. You know what the figures showed, don't you? God had given us back through those scholarships much more money than we had given to the building fund!

I am not going to suggest that God always does a monetary match for our gifts to Him. Sometimes the blessings are more intangible—and more wonderful. I can only share our story and say that Teresa and I understand what R. G. LeTourneau, inventor of the world's largest earth moving machines, once said about giving. He said, "God shovels it out, and I shovel it back; but God has a bigger shovel." He does indeed!

11.

God and Chocolate

Even after your kids are grown, they continue to offer you opportunities to smile. Last week it was our younger daughter, Megan's, turn to make us laugh as we shared her "good fortune."

She is living in Louisville, Kentucky, now, hoping to find a teaching position for the fall. She had saved up money from her last semester's temporary teaching job in Lewis County to take care of her summer expenses, but her budget is pretty tight.

She thought she had received her last check for her semester's work, but to our surprise—and her delight—another check arrived in the mail last Tuesday. Of course, it came to our Grayson address. Teresa called her that evening to give her the good news.

Megan had just worked her first day at her summer job with Godiva's Chocolates. For the unfamiliar, Godiva's Chocolates sells the most decadent and delectable array of chocolate candies in the world at a premium price. Part of her job that first day was to get familiar with the product, eating as many different varieties as she could! The theory, of course, is you can't sell what you don't know or like. So Meg spent the afternoon eating chocolate truffles, chocolate-covered strawberries, cream-filled chocolates and other Godiva specialties. Being a confirmed chocoholic like the rest of her family, it wasn't a hard job.

When Teresa informed her over the phone that another month's paycheck had arrived, she was ecstatic.

"God is so good, Mom," she exclaimed. "This has been the best day of my life. Here, this unexpected check arrives and I have been sitting around eating chocolate all afternoon!"

In our Meg's book, it doesn't get any better than that. I've laughed a dozen times as I have replayed their conversation in my mind. Yes, Megan, God is good—even on days when the check is still in the mail and there's no chocolate to eat.

12.

Tasteless Sin

I have to admit that I do not always hear well. They tell us that we humans are born with the capacity to hear sounds that are pitched from 20 to 20,000 hertz (cycles per second). I am not sure what my current range is, but it is considerably less than that.

But sometimes my inability to hear distinctly leads to serendipitous results. Let me give you an example.

I listen to music on my portable CD player sometimes when I am out walking. One of my favorite artists is country singer Faith Hill. I guess I like her especially because she has a striking resemblance to our daughter, Mandi, and their voices are very similar. Personally, I think Mandi sounds better. (You knew I would say that, didn't you?)

Well, anyway, I like to listen to Faith Hill. With Mandi in Nashville, I miss her so much at times that it is just comforting to listen to Faith and think of Mandi.

I was listening to a song from one of Faith's albums recently that is religious in nature. It is entitled "There Will Come a Day." One of the lines of the chorus begins, "Every knee will bow and sin will have no trace."

Like I said, I don't hear so well. What I thought Faith was singing on the second phrase was "sin will have no *taste*." I went around singing it that way for several days until I finally listened closely enough to get it right!

I have to tell you, however, that I like my mistaken version better. One of the problems with temptation in this world is that sin is so tasty! It excites the mind and appeals to the senses in such a way that we must exercise constant vigilance to avoid falling. Satan works overtime, it seems, to see to it that sin's appearance is always delightful and delicious.

What a wonderful thought that someday sin will lose its power to tantalize and titillate. It will become as insipid to us as bland and tasteless gruel. Our daily battle with temptation will be over. What a day that will be!

13.

Over the Rainbow

It is one my favorite CDs. Mandi sent it to me a few years ago, telling me the story of the artist, Eva Cassidy, who had died tragically of bone cancer at the age of thirty-three. It was only after her death that she was "discovered." Her albums have gone platinum, and listening to her sing just one song gets you hooked. Her voice has a pristine clearness and haunting beauty that is quite unlike anyone's that I have ever heard before.

My favorite cut on the album is her rendition of "Over the Rainbow." Her soulful voice and tremendous range make her presentation of Judy Garland's signature song a classic anew. I listen to it often as I travel in my car from place to place. And sometimes I think of the words.

The song speaks of a place where dreams come true, where *troubles melt like lemon drops*. How ironic it is that the little girl who sang that song originally, Judy Garland as Dorothy in *The Wizard of Oz*, never seemed to realize its fulfillment in her life. Garland was only 47 when she died of an "accidental" overdose of barbiturates in the spring of 1969. The exuberance and innocence of her film role stood in stark contrast to her troubled personal life of five marriages and seemingly constant turmoil.

She could sing the song, but she couldn't produce its effect in her life. Evidently her troubles, instead of melting like lemon drops, had accumulated to the point that life became unbearable.

The truth is that troubles generally are much too recalcitrant in life for any of us to simply find them melting like lemon drops. We needed something else or someone else to help us through those difficult times that a twenty-first century world presents to us. I wish Judy Garland knew that. I hope that Eva Cassidy did.

God sent His Son not only to save us for eternity, but also to make life here a joy—even in the midst of troubles. Jesus said in John 10:10 (KJV), "I am come that they might have life, and that they might have it more abundantly." Regardless of our circumstances, that abundant life is available if we are willing to surrender our lives to Him. Such a life is not "somewhere over the rainbow;" it is here and now. I hope you've found it!

14.

It Hurts So Good

The nagging pain is back, but I am feeling good about it today, not that I am a big fan of pain or particularly stoic in the face of it. It starts in my neck and radiates down my right shoulder. It wakes me up in the night almost anytime I try to roll over in my sleep, but I welcome it this morning as I face my first day back in the office after a visit to Nashville.

It is Nashville that causes the pain. Oh, not specifically Nashville, but rather the events that transpire when we go there now to visit Chris, Mandi, and our new grandchild,

Maizy Song Rioux. Granddad and Nana LeMaster always fight over who is good to feed Maizy and sometimes I am fortunate enough to win out and have the privilege.

And that's the problem causing the pain, feeding Maizy. Being left-handed, I have to hold her in my right arm with the bottle in my left hand in order to accomplish the task. I wouldn't call Maizy a fussy eater, but she takes her own good time in getting the four or five ounces of Similac down that each feeding requires. And, of course, there is the obligatory burping that is necessary after each two ounces. As a result, a bottle takes thirty to forty-five minutes, and with each feeding session my less used right shoulder gets sorer and sorer.

But I wouldn't miss this pain for the world! As I feed our first little grandchild, she looks up at me with big, bright brown eyes that seem to be peering into my soul. I stare back with the same intensity, marveling at this little wonder that has so pleasantly changed our lives.

A few weeks away from Nashville will cause the pain to subside and my sleep to become sounder. But, to be totally honest with you, I would rather have the pain. I am beginning to understand what the Proverbs' writer meant when he penned the words of 17:6, "Children's children are the crown of old men." As I thank God for my many blessings on this Tuesday morning, none seems greater at the moment than my sore shoulder. Really!

15.

It's A Boy!

To say that we were unprepared for the first little boy in our immediate family would be an understatement. Not that Chris and Mandi had failed to plan for a second child after Maizy had reached 18 months—they were both determined that their little girl would not grow up alone if God would bless them with another baby. And not that Kai Merit Rioux was premature either. Mandi was only in her thirty-eighth week of gestation at his birth, but the mandated C-section took place precisely on the day planned.

No, the issue was that this particular branch of the LeMaster and Messer family trees had absolutely no experience with little boys, only little girls. Teresa and I had a delightful time in rearing our two daughters, Mandi and Megan. I say delightful and I mean it. Both of our girls were what I would call "easy" children with temperaments that made our job as parents simple and straightforward. Then came Maizy, our first grandchild. I will admit that she is a little bit more complicated than our girls were, but still is easy to manage because of her gender and grace.

But our first grandson has been a different story! Being inexperienced with rearing little boys, let me share some lessons I am learning about the differences in the two genders of the human species as Kai celebrates his second birthday this month.

Little girls communicate very well by talking and verbalization. Little boys communicate mainly by hitting, throwing, or pulling hair. Kai is a more than proficient talker for a two-year old, but sees no need to use words when physical force or projectiles are much more effective.

Little girls will sit at the table and enjoy eating their favorite foods. Little boys believe that food is to be worn or thrown on the floor. There is never a question as to where Kai has been sitting at the table. The question is, generally, do we clean up him or the mess on the floor beneath him first.

Little girls love clothes and accessorizing and get upset when they get dirty. Little boys love dirt and mud and creating indelible stains on whatever they are wearing. Kai, I don't believe, has ever outgrown anything. After one or two wearings, his clothes are generally rejected by even Goodwill.

Little girls love to have play dates with their friends and enjoy socializing very much. Little boys think friends are really enemies in disguise that make good punching bags. A play date for Kai with his young friends generally requires all parents present, a padded room, and a referee.

Little girls hate creepy, crawly things. Little boys think they are delicious. Truthfully, Kai loves insects, spiders, and bugs, especially the crunchy ones!

I could go on, but I think you get the point. Of course, I am given to hyperbole in my comparisons, but only mildly so. He's a handful, but a wonderful handful. With his little blue spectacles and his million-dollar smile, he has an amazing ability of melting the hearts of his Nana and Granddad especially.

Yes, perhaps we were unprepared for the challenge of a little boy in our family, but we wouldn't miss this opportunity for the world! Truly, Heavenly Father, our children are a blessing, but our "grandchildren are like a crown" (Proverbs 17:6, NIRV).

16.

My Son Is Drunk?

I n the mid-1980s when we were ministering in Ironton, the phone rang one morning at 3 a.m. I stumbled out of bed and walked across the room and reached for the receiver, wondering what church crisis was awaiting me on the other end of the line. With such a large congregation, it was not at all unusual to get such calls in the middle of the night.

But my mental guesses as to the nature of the call weren't even close. I heard a voice saying to me, "Reverend LeMaster, this is the Ironton police department. We have your son in custody. He's drunk and is tearing up the place. Would you please come and get him." The background noise was indeed the loud yells of a young man who seemed out of control.

Being jolted from a deep sleep, my mind was not really working too well. I was trying to process what was being said, but was doing so rather slowly. So I thought to myself, *"Oh, no, my son is drunk and tearing up the jail!"*

It was about at this point that I woke up enough to realize, *"Wait a minute, I don't have a son!"* My relief was followed immediately with major irritation at whoever was propagating this ruse and pretending to be the preacher's kid. I quickly and much more politely than I felt, explained the situation to the officer and hung up the phone.

To this day, I have no clue as to the identity of the young man who, in the midst of his inebriation, decided to play a trick on the preacher. I have always assumed it was probably the son of one of our members or attendees, but I guess I will never know for sure.

But sometimes I wonder if maybe it was a cry for help rather than a cruel attempt at humor. In retrospect, perhaps I should have gotten dressed and gone to the jail and talked to my "son." Calling his bluff would probably have sobered him up in a hurry!

PART II — THINGS

One of my favorite college professors was Donald Nash, who not only was a great teacher, but also an accomplished author. His published works include several books and hundreds of essays written for our church movement's periodicals. Dr. Nash was a stickler when it came to the proper writing style on required term papers for his classes. One of his cardinal rules was that you were never allowed to use the word "thing" or "things" in submitting assignments. He often emphasized, "There is always a better word for what you are describing than 'thing.'"

Hopefully I have not violated his principle in the text articles in this book, but I just had to use the word to head the introduction for this particular selection of stories. Although it is not a perfect fit, "things" describes best what I attempted to write about in this grouping.

I am not much of an abstract thinker, getting most of my inspiration in life from simple themes—people, places, and, yes, things. From combs to credit cards to crayons, I have found myself intrigued and prompted to put pen to paper by some of the most mundane objects existing in my world.

Perhaps the day will arrive when I will leave my concrete subjects and move on to loftier abstract concerns, but I doubt it. At this point in my life it is just too much fun to talk and write about "things." Sorry, Dr. Nash!

1.

Combs!

I am feeling smug and rather proud of myself this morning. Last night I solved a problem that has annoyed me for a long time. I will admit to you that it was a very small problem, but it is one that has cost me time, money and a great deal of frustration!

The problem? Our bathroom vanity comb-eater. Well, it is not really a comb-eater, but that's about the best way I can describe it. There is a small opening between the wall and the Formica top of our downstairs bathroom vanity. You comb your hair in a hurry, drop the comb on the sink, somebody pushes it to the side, and, presto, the comb-eater has it! The comb falls down through the one quarter inch opening and is gone.

Nothing you can do about it, I have thought, but complain at the girls (my wife and two daughters) for letting it happen. (We will not discuss the combs that I have lost with this process!) Complain and then go out and buy a couple more combs and plead with them not to let it happen again. But it always does, and last night we were combless once more.

But I am comb rich this morning! In desperation, I took a coat hanger and bent it appropriately. I then threaded it through the quarter inch opening at the bottom of the vanity where it meets the floor and the wall. And I started pulling out combs! Eighteen of them in all!! After soaking them in hot water and disinfectant overnight, they are as good as new.

What's the point? For over a year, I have fussed and fumed over a problem that was solvable in less than fifteen minutes. I have griped and complained and cajoled and pleaded, but done nothing concrete to address the real issue.

When I stopped complaining and decided to take action, the problem was solved.

I am reminded of the time in the Old Testament when the children of Israel were complaining to God as they stood before the Red Sea. Pharaoh's army was closing in behind them. They were whining and doing nothing. And God told Moses, in essence, "Tell the people to stop crying and start moving!" (Exodus 14:15). They stepped forward and the Red Sea parted. The solution came when they were finally willing to take action.

What personal problem are you worrying about but not really addressing? Do something! You may be surprised how quickly God brings a solution.

2.

Permanent

Women of the world owe a great debt to Charles Nestle, and it has absolutely nothing to do with chocolate. Nestle was the German-born hairstylist who was determined to perfect a wave that could properly be called permanent. In his first experiment, he baked off all but one lock of a woman's head. But Nestle was jubilant—the one lock curled, permanently! His perfected process used a chemical solution and took six hours. It would change the entire hairdressing industry.

But permanents are not permanent. A hairdresser friend explained to me some time ago that they will last from a few days to perhaps three months, according to the texture of the hair and how "tight" the hair is wound. How can anything that lasts just three months be called "permanent?" Seems to me there are other things in life that beg the same question.

How many permanent addresses have you had in your lifetime? According to my calculations, Teresa and I have had at least ten in our thirty-nine plus years of marriage. The forms we fill out for tax, census, and other purposes always call for a permanent address, but the reality is that no such place exists in this world!

Then, there are those folks with permanent disabilities. You know what I am talking about, don't you? Following a "terrible" injury and seemingly endless litigation with the government, a monthly stipend is awarded for a bad back. Amazingly, a few months later the individual is seen lifting eighty-pound sacks of flour into the bed of a truck! A miracle?

Hardly. In our society, for many at least, permanent injuries are simply not permanent.

I could go on, but I think you get my point. Almost all of the things that we call permanent in our world are in reality temporary at best. And yet our souls cry out for something that is lasting, something rock solid that does not change with the changing times—something to which we can anchor ourselves during the storms of life. The good news is that something of such permanence exists! The prophet Isaiah said it best, "The grass withers and the flowers fall, but the word of our God stands forever" (Isaiah 40:8).

God's word is permanent. His truth has always existed and always will. You won't wake up tomorrow and find that the rules are different. In a capricious, constantly changing world, I take great comfort in this reality. In fact, I have anchored my soul to the Christ of this immutable Word. I hope you have as well.

3.

What Time Is It?

It is time for a battery replacement for my watch. I have noticed the past week or so that when I check its time with other reliable clocks and watches that I am losing a couple minutes or so each day. I immediately stop and reset it, but the next day I'm back in the same predicament. So, today or tomorrow, I will buy a new battery for three or four dollars and then I will be back in the time-telling business.

I like my watch. I guess you could say it has sentimental value to me. It was given to me by a pharmacist friend about a dozen years ago for some help I had given him. He was studying for his doctorate in pharmacology at UK and was having trouble with statistics. He and I would meet in my office very early a couple of days a week to work on his homework problems. He passed the course, received his doctorate, and rewarded me with the watch. In case you are wondering, it's a Timex. It probably cost about $25 and has been my constant companion for the past decade. When I look at it sometimes, I can't help but think of "Dr. Dan" and those early mornings working on probabilities and analyses of variance.

But that's not why I wear the watch. I wear the watch because it has always been a very reliable timepiece, except when it's needed a battery replacement. Which prompts me to ask my question for the day: what is the difference between a Timex and a Rolex?

If your answer to the question is "about $9, 975," you are right! I know some folks (and they are fine people) who wear Rolexes, and I have found that my watch keeps time as accurately as theirs. When their Rolexes read 10:25 a.m., my Timex does, too. When they wake up confused in the middle of the night and want to know what time it is, they look at their watches and get a very accurate answer. I can do the same thing with my Timex. When they have an important appointment and need to be on time, they can trust their Rolexes. And I can trust my Timex.

Please don't think I am putting down Rolexes or the people who wear them. Truth is, if Dan had given me a Rolex, I would probably still be wearing it today. But the end result would be the same, a reliable timepiece that "takes a lickin' and keeps on tickin'!"

What are you trying to say, Phil? Quality is important, but extravagance is generally a waste we indulge in for the other reasons. Think about this the next time you are tempted to buy the most expensive brand.

4.

Platinum

One wintry morning several years ago the phone rang, and immediately the precise diction of the caller tipped me off that it was a business solicitation. After a couple of opening niceties, the spiel came.

"Mr. LeMaster, I am calling to say that you are pre-approved for our new platinum Discover Card!"

Quickly I deflated the solicitor's enthusiasm by responding, "I am sorry. One of my New Year's resolutions is not to obtain any more credit cards. Thank you for calling."

I went back to my chores, but could not seem to get the call off my mind. Like most of you, we use to receive frequent phone and mail solicitations for credit cards. Our then teenage younger daughter Megan, whose credit history was shorter than a "give-me" putt, got almost weekly mailings inviting her to charge it with Visa or Master Card Platinum.

That was what stuck in my mind—the platinum idea. Gold is no longer good enough when it comes to credit cards. Only platinum cards will do now for the really discerning consumer.

Platinum, so I am told, is the world's newest, rarest metal, discovered only in the 1600s. How rare? All the platinum ever mined would occupy less than twenty-five cubic feet. More precious than gold, some would say. Recent metal prices had platinum at $1100 per ounce compared to gold's $912 per ounce. Not long ago, the local newspaper carried a front page article about the wave of thefts of automobiles' catalytic converters in our area. The reason? Each converter contains a small amount of platinum that will bring up to $100 on the black market.

Platinum is obviously all the rage today. You have not really made it in the music industry any more when your recording has gone golden (500,000 units). You must have a platinum album (1,000,000 units) to really be considered a top draw. Platinum wedding bands are being touted as the superior choice when deciding to "tie the knot." And the day will probably come when we award four medals to Olympic competitors instead of the present three. Gold medals will go to mere second-place finishers. The winners will have platinum draped around their necks.

Call me old-fashioned, but you will never replace the "gold standard" as far as I am concerned. To me, a man's word can be as good as gold, but no better. And a proper silence will always be golden in my book. And, please, no platinum streets in heaven! Gold will do just fine!!

5.

Green Side Up!

Anybody who knows me knows well that I am no mechanical genius. A *faux pas* I made several years ago illustrates the point perfectly. The rearview mirror had fallen off of our 1991 Lumina. It is a simple problem to fix and one that a third-grader could handle. I got the little re-gluing kit from a local auto supply store and carefully went about reading the instructions before doing the repair. I wanted to do it right!

There is only one major step. You re-glue the metal piece or button that holds the mirror in place to the windshield.

This piece is beveled on one side so that the mirror will slide down over it. All you have to do is make sure you glue the beveled side to the windshield. A friend who had replaced a mirror a few days before even reminded me of this fact before I tackled the job.

You guessed it. I glued the non-beveled side to the windshield. Then I let it set overnight so that it would be sure to hold. When I went to attach the mirror the next morning, I discovered my mistake. And you talk about a product that works—the metal button was super glued in place!

I won't tell you how I finally got the button loose (or how many man-hours it took), but the experience left me feeling that I had secured a place in the Mechanically Declined Hall of Fame.

It reminded me of that old joke about the man who had some less than intelligent workers sodding his front lawn. From time to time he would yell out the window, "Green side up!" Someone needed to be yelling at me, "Beveled side in!"

You're laughing at me and I am laughing, too. The simple truth is that I am not gifted in the area of mechanics. Well, let's be honest, I am a mechanical moron. Changing the oil in my car is about as complicated a task as I can handle. But that's okay. I realize that God has given me other talents that I can use in serving him.

The real tragedy would be if I spent much time lamenting my mechanical ineptitude instead of using the abilities God has given me to His glory. God has gifted us all differently. Our task is to identify these gifts and get busy using them in the work of the Kingdom. From now on I will leave auto repair jobs, even the simple ones, to someone else.

6.

Shattered Dreams?

It just shattered. No forceful blows, no errant objects thrown against it, no body slams. I went into the kitchen one winter evening and heard a crinkling sound coming from the direction of the French patio doors in our Grayson, Kentucky, home. I pulled back the curtain and was shocked to see that the glass in one door was fragmenting into a million pieces.

The glass was still in place and looked rather artistic with its mosaic design, especially when the sun caught it just right. Of course, removal was necessary, calling for a whole new set of doors—frames, hardware and all.

I was questioned by our insurance adjuster and a repairman at some length.

"What happened?" they asked.

"Nothing," I replied.

"Nothing?" They responded.

"Nothing," I said with more emphasis the second time.

Of course, I didn't really mean nothing. Obviously, one look at the door and you knew something had happened, but you understand my answer, don't you? I mean, to the best of our knowledge, neither Teresa nor I had done anything to produce the unfortunate outcome.

That's the way life is sometimes, is it not? Difficulties and problems appear out of thin air with no obvious origin. Maybe it is a health concern we wake up with one morning. We went to bed feeling good, but daybreak finds us writhing in pain. We search our minds as to what caused it, but come up empty. But still the ache persists.

Perhaps our adult child gets into trouble. We rehearse our child-rearing practices and try to find the reason, but are clueless at the end. Or we give our employer our best efforts for a dozen years and then receive a pink slip one Friday afternoon. We try to figure out how we went so quickly from being an asset to being a liability, but no answer comes.

What do we do when our neat world of cause-and-effect breaks down? When our question "why" bounces off the walls and reverberates back unanswered? Well, I will tell you what we did with our patio doors. We laughed at our bizarre accident, replaced the doors, and thanked God for good insurance coverage.

Please don't think that I am trying to trivialize the "uncaused" problem you may be facing just now. The simple truth is that we often waste too much precious time and energy asking why, when we should simply deal with the issue. Ask God for direction, make your decision, and move on. God can be trusted. He will carry you through to other side if you will let Him.

7.

Ladybugs

Seen any ladybugs recently? I bet you have. Due to the warm weather, they are swarming in unusually large numbers this fall. And making a real nuisance of themselves! Besides clustering on doors, ceilings, and walls, they give off an odor that rates somewhere between dirty socks and rotten eggs as to its "stink quotient."

You've tried almost everything to get rid of them, right? Insecticides. Forget it. You might as well throw the bottle at them for all the good it does. Squashing them. That's a real mistake, isn't it? What color is the stain on your carpet?

Vacuuming them up. That's the LeMaster favorite method of disposal, although you better empty the canister immediately or prepare for a surprise the next time you houseclean!

In spite of our hatred of the little critters, did you know that they are really a blessing to our world? They are probably the best natural pesticide ever created by God. An adult ladybug will eat 5,000 aphids during its lifetime—and aphids are the real nuisance. Believe it or not, our country has imported ladybugs on more than one occasion to help us deal with the true pests that attack fruit trees and garden crops.

In fact, if you are very enterprising, I can tell you something else you can do with your ladybugs. Sell them! According to those who know, you can get about $16.50 for a garden size allotment of approximate 1,500 ladybugs (about the number we have had in our living room this last week).

Now you are expecting me to come up with some theological truth before this article is finished, aren't you? Well, did you know where the ladybug got its name?

During the Middle Ages, swarms of pests were destroying crops and farmers prayed to the Virgin Mary for help. Soon after, ladybugs came and ate the bad pests and saved the crops. The farmers began calling the bugs, "Beetles of Our Lady." Eventually they became known simply as ladybugs.

So here's a thought. When you see a ladybug, think of Mary. And thinking of Mary, think of her sinless Son, Jesus Christ. And remember that just as these tiny bugs eradicate the world of countless pests, He is capable of removing countless sins from our lives. With this Jesus in your life, the devil loses his power to "bug" you. You knew that was coming, didn't you? So thank God for ladybugs and praise Him for His Son who helps us defeat our ultimate pest, Satan.

8.

Lowell's Syndrome

The landings and explorations of the *Spirit* and *Opportunity* rovers on Mars remind me of the "discovery" of the canals of Mars by the great astronomer, Sir Percival Lowell, more than a century ago.

Lowell, encouraged by the findings of an Italian astronomer, spent the last years of his life squinting into the eyepiece of his giant telescope in Arizona, mapping the channels and canals he saw. He was convinced that the canals were proof of intelligent life on the planet, possibly an older but wiser race than humanity.

Because of his stature in the scientific community, Lowell's observations gained wide acceptance. After all, who would dare contradict the greatest astronomer of his day?

But as the two rovers continue to search the surface of the red planet, of course, no such canals will be found. We have known for many years now, from earlier probes that mapped the entire planet, that Lowell was mistaken. And we think we know why.

Lowell suffered from a rare eye disease that made him see the blood vessels in his own eyes. The Martian "canals" he saw were nothing more than the bulging veins of his eyeballs! Today this malady is known as "Lowell's syndrome."

I know some people, don't you, who have the spiritual equivalent of this particular disease. They have a great ability to detect and enumerate the flaws in the lives of other people. With amazing acuity, they are able to see the sins of their neighbors, sometimes even to the point of reading their neighbor's minds (as in "I know why he said that" or "I know why she did that.").

In reality, these critical folks are engaging in a very dangerous practice. Jesus warns us in the Sermon on the Mount, Matthew 7:1-3, about judging others when the speck in our neighbor's eye is not nearly as glaring as the plank in our own eye. Lowell would have been wise to put down his telescope and look in the mirror. Perhaps we should do so as well.

9.

Tees-A-Plenty

One recent afternoon I went golfing by myself. I am trying to get into shape, and I find that walking eighteen holes on hilly terrain when the temperature gauge reads 85°F degrees is quite helpful, regardless of my score!

At the first hole, I got a couple of balls out of my golf bag and looked for some tees. Usually I have hundreds, scattered around in every pocket of the bag. But on this afternoon, I was almost teeless. I could only find four, and I knew that I would probably need at least a dozen. The temperature had already hit 90°F and the walk back to the clubhouse was too far. I decided to start my round anyway and to try to survive by looking for tees along the way.

Now, I always end the round with fewer tees than I had at the beginning. You break them, you lose them, or they just see a chance to escape from the golf bag and disappear. You know, like one tee saying to another, "He's hunting for a lost ball. Let's get out of here!" Sort of like the way socks escape from clothes' dryers.

But on this particular day, for the first time I can remember in recent history, I had my eyes open and I was looking for tees. At every tee box before I hit, I would scoured the area and search for them. I just knew that I would run out before the round was over. Well, you know what happened, of course. By the end of the round, I had a pocket full of tees I had picked up along the way. Not only did I not run out, I had replenished my supply for the next outing.

I suppose there are several applications which could be made from this little story, but the obvious one is that there are many things in life which would enrich us if we only had our eyes open to them.

God's blessings are multitudinous for those people who are looking for them, but they are often missed by those of us who have our eyes closed. With the Psalmist we need to pray, "Open my eyes that I might see." (Psalm 119:18).

10.

Tommy

Tommy's home again and his family has not killed the fatted calf, but they certainly are rejoicing.

Tommy is seven years old and a member of my brother Joe's family. To say that he is precocious would be an understatement. He started to school when he was barely a year old and has returned every year since. Believe it or not, he goes to teach rather than to learn. An amazing instructor, students seldom forget the lessons in zoology that he shares with them.

But on July 12th of this year, sometime in the night, Tommy stealthily left the warm confines of his home. Joe and Mella, and especially their young son, Jasper, were very upset at his disappearance. The concern was not only for Tommy's welfare, but also for others that he might encounter on his wayward journey.

What made him want to leave? Nobody knows for sure. Maybe he was hungry and looking for a midnight snack. Perhaps he was bored and interested in seeing the big, wide world. Most likely, he just saw the opportunity was his and vanished.

You can imagine the anxiety of Joe's family as they searched for Tommy and worried about his well-being. Since he was so ill equipped for such an expedition, they wondered aloud if foul play perhaps had made an end to his young life.

The first week passed and then the second. Hopes of Tommy returning decreased with the dawning of each new day. But then, on July 27th, Tommy reappeared just as suddenly as he had disappeared!

Evidently he had found that the big, wide world was not for him. Bedraggled and hungry, he had made his way back home. And rather than scolding or reprimanding him, Joe and Mella welcomed him without any qualms or questions. There will be no discipline, only a special meal of perhaps four live mice.

That meal may not sound exciting to you, but for a ball python like Tommy, it is just about as good as it gets. You and I would agree that he does not deserve it, but then we don't love Tommy like Joe and his family do. Love will make you do some amazing things, won't it?

11.

Vanity Plates

Teresa and I enjoyed a vacation at historic Williamsburg, VA, recently. I am not the most astute observer in the world, but it became apparent very quickly in our daily drives that vanity plates seem to be "in" in that commonwealth. I saw more vanity license plates on cars in one week there than in a year in middle Tennessee.

I wasn't surprised, therefore, when the newspaper mentioned that Virginia has more vanity plates than any other state in the union. Of the 9.3 million vanity plate owners in the United States, one out of ten is a Virginian. According to the Association of Motor Vehicle Administrators, 16 percent of the drivers in Virginia have vanity plates. At the other end of the spectrum is Texas, where less than 1 percent of registered vehicles are "vanitized." I guess when your state is that big, you don't have to brag!

Before you and I start to think of Virginians as our country's egomaniacs, I should point out that such plates only cost $10 extra there. My vote for the "Carly Simon You're So Vain" award would go to those 1.3 million folks (most actual number for a state) from Illinois who purchased vanity plates at $78 per pop. Now, that is paying a price to make a statement!

Although I am too tight (I would like to think unvain, but...) to purchase vanity plates, I confess that I enjoy them nonetheless. Like the urology specialist back in my home territory of Appalachia whose car was tagged I HLP U P. Not so humorous, in my estimation, is the dentist's plate that reads OPN WYD. Ouch!

How about some famous people's license plates? Did you know that Liberace's plate read 88KEYS? Lawrence Welk's was appropriately stamped A1 AN A2. G. Gordon Liddy, one of Nixon's associates during his scandalous administration, has H2O GATE on his Corvette, so I am told.

No doubt, my favorite vanity plate is the one that our daughter Megan pointed out to me on our trip home from Louisville over Thanksgiving. I had seen it on another car in another state once before, but it still touches my heart as a believer. It reads simply 4GVN. When I cut to the chase in my life, the grace of God is the most defining truth about Phil LeMaster. As I look at the fumbles and failures of my past, it still overwhelms to know that my Heavenly Father's love is greater than my sin. I will spend the rest of my days being amazed at His forgiveness.

12.

Raw Umber and Burnt Sienna

One late October day, I drove from our home in Grayson over to Lewis County, Kentucky, to see my mother and do some work for my brothers. It was interesting to note the change in the colors of the leaves as I traveled the AA highway. The beautiful reds, oranges, and yellows of early autumn had disappeared, and in their place were darker hues that were much less pleasing to the eye.

In trying to pinpoint the colors, I found myself thinking of crayons and of the hues in the boxes of sixty-four which seemed to match up with the Eastern Kentucky hills' late fall foliage.

"Raw umber!" I thought to myself. Actually "burnt umber" is what I thought, but a phone call to Crayola convinced me that they had never produced such a color. Raw umber and burnt sienna were two of the colors we ignored in our Crayola "big boxes." The reds and yellows, and even the golds and silvers, were pulled out of the box and used over and over again.

Raw umber and burnt sienna, however, would lie there, patiently waiting their turn, but never being used. Those two dull earth tones were just a waste of space in the box, it seemed. In fact, when I called Crayola, the official response was that they retired raw umber in 1991. But God needs them and uses them! There comes a time each fall when He presses them into service and they become the main players on His autumnal canvas. With a divine artist's touch, He erases the brilliant colors and repaints the hills with somber hues that are dark and mysterious.

It shouldn't surprise us that God has a use for every color. You may not believe it, but I am convinced that eventually we would tire of the brilliant reds, yellows, and oranges if no other colors were allowed on nature's canvas. The changing seasons and changing colors are simply a part of God's grace to man in my estimation, adding to the wonder of the world that He has given us to enjoy.

The somber hues teach us an important lesson as well. Maybe you are more of a raw umber than a brilliant red. That's okay. Just as surely as God has a place for the showy crimson, He has a need for the humble brown in His kingdom. Perhaps you are a burnt sienna and you are envious of the bright oranges and yellows that dazzle with amazing giftedness. You shouldn't be. God can use only so many brilliant colors; His canvas and His church demand the balance and stability that only the muted tones can provide.

As a raw umber or a burnt sienna, our job is not to lament our minor status in God's palette, but to find where He wants to use us on His canvas and get busy. When we do, we will discover the joy of being a part of the Master Artist's design for His kingdom.

PART III—SCHOOL

It was always one of the most exciting days of the summer for me as I was growing up. Mom would come home from a shopping expedition and present each of her five youngest boys with their fall school clothes: flannel shirts, jeans, and a new pair of brogans. Fashions come and go and I am not about to suggest that those particular outfits were ever "in," but they triggered the thought in my mind that school was about to start for another year.

I loved school! I realize that sounds weird or crazy to most readers, but I had the very fortunate experience of growing up in a positive learning environment that whetted my appetite for knowledge. God had gifted me with the ability to learn and that gift was greatly facilitated by the blessing of excellent teachers especially in my early years. I owe a great debt to Miss Vergne, Mr. Talley, Mrs. Bays, and others who patiently encouraged me in my fledgling academic pursuits.

There is a tendency for some in our country to look with disdain on any product or process that originates in that portion of the United States known as Appalachia. I have seen the documentaries and heard the rhetoric. We are portrayed as not only impoverished in substance, but also in mind. I could not disagree more! I wouldn't trade my training at Garrison Consolidated Elementary and Lewis County High School for an education at any of the finest prep schools in Boston, New York City, or London.

Funny things happen in the classroom and elsewhere in the school setting. The lessons of the structured curricula are often eclipsed by what we learn on the periphery. Although I have hopefully stored much of the classroom knowledge somewhere, the stories I remember best took place on the playground, in the gymnasium and the cafeteria, or walking in the halls between classes. I share some of these incidents on the following pages.

1.

The Fear Factor

The strong smell of rubbing alcohol in the air was my first warning. Like a Pavlovian dog, my heart began to beat rapidly and beads of sweat broke out on my forehead. I felt a sudden nausea sweep over me. Mrs. Newman was paying a visit to our elementary school!

My near-panic was predictable when you think about it. It had nothing to do with Mrs. Newman's imposing size or her booming voice. It wasn't the fact that she reminded me of Sergeant Carter, Gomer Pyle's nemesis. No, my heart-palpitating fear was due to who Mrs. Newman was, the county health nurse. Her visit to our school could mean only one thing. It was "shot day"; time for inoculations again!

As seven-year old second grade boys, her presence presented a particular dilemma for Roger Caldwell and me especially. We knew the girls would all cry and we knew that several of the namby-pamby boys would as well. But Roger and I were the strong guys in class and everybody knew it. We were the ones who hit the most home runs during recess and carried the ball in tackle football. We were tough and now it was the time for us to uphold our reputation.

Our class was finally called to the gymnasium for our injections. Roger and I lined up at the back, bragging about how shots didn't worry us in the least. The only problem was that as the line got shorter, my heart became larger in my throat. The pungent smell of the antiseptic alcohol got stronger and stronger, and Mrs. Newman's powerful voice made me want to stuff some of the cotton on the tables in my ears.

I looked at Roger. He was still playing the tough guy and doing rather well at it. Several of the girls in line seemed unperturbed and a couple were even laughing. Me? Well, I wanted out of there in the worst way! I knew I couldn't run, even though I'm pretty sure I could have outdistanced Mrs. Newman in a footrace. Finally, when I was fifth or sixth from the front of the line, the tears welled up in my eyes and I cried like a baby!

And, then, it was my turn. With a smile and a kind word, she swabbed my arm with rubbing alcohol and gave the injection. It was over before I even knew it, and the pain was less than a bee sting on a bare-footed boy's sole on a summer afternoon.

I had gotten all worked up over almost nothing and embarrassed myself before my classmates. I had wasted ten dollars' worth of adrenalin on a ten-cent problem!

Have you ever done it? Stewed and fretted and worried about an impending issue only to learn that the experience was much less traumatic than the fretting? What a waste of time and emotional energy!

Erma Bombeck said it well, "Worry is like a rocking chair; it gives you something to do, but doesn't take you anywhere." The apostle Paul suggests a better option than worry in Philippians 4:6, "Do not be anxious about anything, but in everything, by prayer and petition, with thanksgiving, present your requests to God."

We can fret and worry or we can pray, but we can't do both simultaneously. The choice is ours.

2.

Lessons from a Cheese Cube

It was one of those learning experiences you would just as soon read about in the life of someone else. I was a sixth grader at Garrison Consolidated School. Delores Bays was my teacher for the second year in a row; she taught the fifth and sixth grades together. A strictly business type of teacher, she allowed absolutely no misbehavior from her students.

It was chili day in the lunchroom cafeteria. With boring regularity, the school lunch menu repeated every ten days or so. Chili day also meant that you received a peanut butter sandwich, carrot and celery sticks, and cubes of American cheese. The cubes were a real temptation to some of us boys, especially when we were not too hungry. They were excellent projectiles to toss at unwary friends or enemies.

I am not sure exactly how it happened, but I made the totally unwise decision to throw a cube of cheese at someone. The memory seems to unfold in slow motion when I think about it now. In mid-toss, Mrs. Eakins, our principal, opened the "spy door" from her office and caught me in the act. Now, if Mrs. Bays was a Nazi storm trooper, Mrs. Eakins was the Fuhrer. She absolutely terrified me. Her yell of "stop that immediately" reverberated off the walls of the cafeteria. I stopped immediately. Sitting like a choir boy the rest of the lunch time, I ate the remainder of my cheese cubes, hoping to destroy any damaging evidence in the process.

I walked back to our classroom like a condemned criminal heading to his execution. I was sure Mrs. Bays was going to kill me. I had embarrassed her in front of the principal, the worst possible offense. In my mind, I was already dividing my worldly goods among my survivors.

Back in our classroom, I waited for the explosion. It never came. Mrs. Bays, a very wise woman who really cared about me, simply said, "Phil, I want you to go to Mrs. Eakins' office and apologize for your behavior."

Well, as you can imagine, flagellation would have been easier. The trip to the principal's office I have somehow blocked from conscious memory. Repression would be Freud's diagnosis.

Needless to say, it marked the end of my cheese-throwing career. It also taught me a very important lesson about accepting responsibility for your behavior. Sometimes when you do something wrong, you are able to make amends via restitution. Sometimes all you can do is to say that you are sorry and change your behavior for the future.

In retrospect, it was one of the most important lessons I ever learned in grade school. It has served me well in life. Thanks, Mrs. Bays.

3.

Stay in the Game

It was the most bizarre end to a basketball game I can remember. We were playing in a grade-school tournament at Tollesboro, Kentucky. In spite of the fact that we were limited in talent, our eighth-grade Garrison Bulldogs were staying close to a rival school from the Tollesboro area.

Our coach, George Smith, was no great lover of referees, particularly one of the two men who was helping to officiate the game that night. I kept getting fouled and going to foul line (in those days you shot free throws on every violation). I made almost every foul shot, but this referee kept calling my foot over the line, nullifying the points! Was I guilty? I didn't think so, nor did Coach Smith.

He reprimanded (that's a mild word) the referee a couple of times, but the calls kept going the other team's way. Finally, Coach had all he could stand.

"Come on, boys," he said, "We're going home."

And with just a couple of minutes left in the second quarter, we walked off the court and to the dressing room. In spite of pleas from the tournament's officials, we dressed into our street clothes and left.

In retrospect, I am not sure that Coach Smith made the right decision that night with his unorthodox move. Certainly, we were getting "homered," and the chances of us getting a legitimate shot at winning were almost nil. But "taking our ball and going home" assured us that we would lose and would be labeled quitters in the eyes of our opposition.

There are times in the game of life when the playing floor does not seem level at all. Satan is a persistent foe who is willing to break every rule in the book in order to destroy our souls and win our eternal damnation. He lies and he cheats and he always has (John 8:44). If you sometimes feel like quitting because of his chicanery, understand that countless saints of God have felt the same way in the past.

But the only way to win is to stay in the game. The apostle Paul summed up his "playing career" in his last letter to his son in the faith, Timothy, when he said, "I have fought the good fight, I have finished the race, I have kept the faith" (II Timothy 4:6). The great apostle to the Gentile's example is worthy of emulation. Let's stay in the game until the very end. Victory awaits us!

4.

My First Flashbulb Memory

On November 22, 1963, in Dallas, Texas, President John F. Kennedy was assassinated. The sad event was the first flashbulb memory of my life and probably the most significant one of that generation. Flashbulb memories, according to psychologists, are those major events in a nation's history that are so overwhelming that every citizen can remember, in vivid detail, where they were and what they were doing when the event occurred.

Can you remember where you were when you first heard of Kennedy's death? I was sitting in a biology class at Lewis County High School near Vanceburg, Kentucky, when suddenly noise came from the classroom intercom system. Then a somber voice was heard, that of Walter Cronkite the famed newscaster stating, "Here is a bulletin from CBS News. From Dallas, Texas, a flash, apparently official: President Kennedy died at 1 p.m. Central Standard Time, 2 p.m., Eastern Standard Time, some thirty-eight minutes ago."

The whole experience took on the nature of surrealism. I simply could not believe it at first. I found myself thinking, "This is somebody's sick joke. President Kennedy couldn't be dead. He is only in his forties. Someone has made a terrible mistake."

But as the afternoon wore on, the awful truth set in. Our President was dead and Camelot was over. With amazing swiftness the hopeful dreams of my generation, spawned by such a vibrant and youthful leader, gave way to the realities of the Vietnam War and the disenchantment of the flower children of the West Coast.

I am reminded of the funeral of King Louis XIV of France. The king had ruled seventy-two years, longer than any monarch in modern European history. He had once declared, "I am the State!" He took delight in the fact that many of his subjects referred to him as Louis the Great. Bishop Massillon, the orator at his funeral, first reached over and snuffed out the single lighted candle on the podium representing the king's life. Then he said simply, "Only God is great."

The bishop's lesson came home to me as a young boy of fifteen in the wake of Kennedy's death. Man, even at his zenith, is transitory. It is wiser to put your trust in something or someone who is eternal. That someone is Jesus who could say, "I am the resurrection and the life. He who believes in me will live, even though he dies" (John 11:25).

5.

A Lesson in Humility

My friends and I opened the Louisville *Courier-Journal* with more than usual interest as we sat in the library at Lewis County High School. It was late November of my senior year, and we had won the biggest basketball game of our careers the Friday night before, beating the Tenth Region powerhouse, Mason County, by 20 points.

We knew it meant that we would probably be rated high in our region by the Liktenhaus poll, but the news was even better than that. Eighteenth in the state! It was there for the entire world to see! The top twenty-five teams in Kentucky high school basketball were always listed in big block letters and there we were: ***18. Lewis County***!

Johnny Swearingen, Roger Brown, and I just sat looking at the ratings, inwardly gloating about our "arrival" as a state basketball power. The Ashland's and Lexington Henry Clay's and Louisville Male's of Kentucky basketball had nothing on us. We were just as good. We knew it and now the paper had confirmed it.

That very week we went to Flemingsburg to play Fleming County in their old and cold gymnasium. Their gym looked more like a swimming pool than a playing court for basketball. You literally had to climb down a ladder to get to the playing floor. In spite of the inclement conditions, we warmed up for the game with considerable enthusiasm, confident of another big win.

I mean, we were eighteenth in the state, weren't we? I envisioned Fleming County's players watching us in warm-ups with fear and trepidation in their hearts. They knew what we had done to Mason County a few days before and they were not nearly as good as the Royals. What would it be, a thirty or forty point victory? Hey, maybe next week we will be in the top ten in the state. Look out, state tournament, here we come!

The game started and it was soon very apparent that Fleming County hadn't read the reports about how good we were. They came ready to play and we did not. Sparing the ugly details, they beat us easily and our stay in the state top twenty-five was over almost before it began.

It was a bitter pill to swallow, but the lesson I learned from the experience was worth it. The Proverbs' writer said it best, "Pride goes before destruction, a haughty spirit before a fall" (16:18). Vigilance and effort born out of humility is necessary if we are going to be winners, both in basketball and life!

6.

My Tobacco Role

The summer before my first year of college, I worked for the Agricultural Stabilization and Conservation Service (ASCS) office in Lewis County doing a job that no longer exists. It was back in the days when tobacco allotments were distributed by acreage rather than by pounds, requiring surveyors to measure each plot to be sure that farmers weren't growing too much. That was my job, and I crisscrossed the county that summer of 1966, going up hills and hollows, paying visits on farmers and their burley crops.

It was an interesting job and helped to teach me quite a bit about human nature. All farmers that summer knew exactly what their allotment size was and most had gone to the trouble to carefully plan their planting. These fields were blissfully trouble-free for the surveyor, with straight rows and squared ends that made my job easy. When I came upon such a tract, I almost always knew that the calculations I made at the end of the job would indicate that the amount of tobacco planted and the allotment allowed were precisely the same.

But there were some fields that were not that way. The rows were less than straight and the ends were uneven. Sometimes the lay of the land dictated such a pattern, but often it seemed that the farmer had just thrown the tobacco plants in the air and let them take root where they landed!

I hated measuring such fields. It was my job to square them up on paper and produce a consistent pattern that would translate into a measurable plot. To be honest, sometimes it required a great deal of imagination to make sense out of such haphazard and careless planting. Invariably, I would find that most of farmers with such fields never had a clue as to whether they were over or under their prescribed allotment allowance.

If they were under in their allotment, they were cheating themselves out of part of their crop, and if they were over, they would have a second visit from an ASCS employee. I would return (or another surveyor) to see them in an even less enjoyable role, that of the tobacco destroyer.

On this second visit, I was required to oversee their destruction of the excess part of their crop. I hated that phase of the job and, of course, farmers hated to see me return! To add insult to injury, they had to pay a pretty steep fee to ASCS to destroy their own tobacco.

My experience that hot, hazy summer over forty years ago really imitates life, doesn't it? Some people plan their lives very carefully, knowing what the requirements are and taking great pains to establish the proper boundaries. As a result, the blessings from God flow. Other folks are careless and carefree, not putting much effort or intentionality into their life plan. The end result is that they cheat themselves out of the real joys of life and find themselves unprepared for the final day of reckoning.

7.

Help from an Atheist

I probably wouldn't be a preacher today if it was not for the first real atheist I ever met. Looking back now, I realize that he was the devil's tool, but God used him to change my life for good more than he would ever suspect.

Dr. Arends was his name and he was an English professor at Morehead State University in the fall of 1966 when I enrolled as a freshman. On our first day on campus, we had taken an English exam for placement. As a result, about thirty of us were allowed to skip the normal grammar classes and take a special literature course instead.

Dr. Arends was the instructor and seemed to relish the opportunity to indoctrinate young minds in the "truth" of life. That "truth" was not that God was dead, but rather that He had never existed in the first place. How that subject matter became the central focus of a freshman English class is probably hard to imagine, but Dr. Arends obviously had an agenda.

Using a book entitled *The World of Ideas*, he worked to hammer home to us misinformed fundamentalists from Appalachia the error of our thinking. A wiry little man with a soft-spoken voice, he was nonetheless pugnacious in his approach to the topic. I can recall him reducing one girl to tears on several occasions as she tried to present her Christian convictions.

At that point in time, I was what I would call "a regular church attending, non-practicing Christian." I knew all of the rules, made most of the proper motions, but in my heart I had little active faith.

Dr. Arends did me a big favor. He forced me to consciously think about what I really believed. He challenged my Christianity in a way that no preacher or Sunday school teacher had ever done. By the end of the semester, I not only was willing to defend my faith; I was also ready to leave the secular university and transfer to Kentucky Christian College to prepare for the ministry.

It is amazing how God can use even the most negative experiences (and it was!) for the good of His children. The seeds of faith had been planted in my life throughout my childhood, but it took an atheistic teacher to cause them to germinate and produce fruit.

Perhaps you are facing a difficult situation or perplexing problem right now in your life. Do you sometimes feel like Satan himself is camped on your doorstep? Don't be surprised if God uses your circumstances to better equip you to do His work. Remember Joseph's words to his brothers, "You intended to harm me, but God intended it for good" (Genesis 50:20).

8.

He Is the Boss of Me!

After my freshman year at Kentucky Christian College, my brother, Mike, invited me to come to Galion, Ohio, where he and his family lived to look for summer work. Fortunately after only a couple of days of job hunting, I was hired by Urban Industries of Ohio, a company that manufactured awnings for mobile homes.

My first and only factory job, I was required to help roll panels, make screened windows, and assemble awning kits for shipping. Work began at 7 a.m., necessitating getting up at 5:45, a time of the morning that I had seldom seen in my teenage years! The small factory had only about twenty workers, most of whom were rough on the edges and laced every sentence with profanity. My boss was Carl Snelcker, a tall, balding man in his late 50s, who said little except when he was chewing me out for the mistakes that I made. It took only about three weeks of work for me to conclude that I thoroughly hated the job.

Even though I had gone to college for a year, this was my first real experience away from home. I became increasingly homesick with every passing day. Before the first month of summer was over, I was ready to quit and go back to Kentucky.

But then one evening while reading the Bible and having my devotional time, I came upon a verse in the New Testament that changed my summer and my life. The verse was Colossians 3:23, where Paul wrote, "Whatever you do, work at it with all your heart, as working for the Lord, not for men."

It was almost like the words leaped off of the page and into my heart. God seemed to be saying to me, "Phil, you are not working for Urban Industries of Ohio. You are not working for Carl Snelcker. You are working for Me!" And, of course, this was true. I was earning money to go back to KCC so I could continue my training to become a minister of the Gospel. It suddenly struck me that any task or job that I endeavored to do deserved my best because my ultimate employer was God.

When I went back on the job the next morning, Urban Industries had an entirely new employee. I began to work at every task with the thought, "I am working for God. I need to do my very best." And I did. When I wasn't working at an assignment given to me by Carl Snelcker, I was sweeping up our work area, rearranging parts in their bins, or assembling extra kits. After a couple of weeks, I was even given a ten-cents an hour raise!

The summer flew by and soon it was time to go back to Kentucky. A younger brother, Rowland, had also worked that summer and worked well. I went to Carl Snelcker and told him that we would be leaving to go back to school at the end of the week. On our final day, he came to us and said, "I just want you boys to know that you will always have a job here if you want it."

The lesson that I learned that summer of 1967 has blessed my life ever since. As a Christian, any endeavor I undertake in this world deserves my best because I am doing it ultimately for my Heavenly Father. Most of all, I want Him to be pleased with my effort. In the process of doing my best, I have also learned that life is a lot more fun!

PART IV — HOME

Although he died in distant Tunis, Africa, and spent much of his life far from its warm confines, John Howard Payne said it well for most of us when he wrote, "Be it ever so humble, there is no place like home."

Of all of my blessings in life, growing up as one of Ned and Hazel LeMaster's kids on a four-acre plot of land near Quincy, Kentucky, goes near the top of the list. The sixth of nine children who lived to adulthood (an older sister, Constance, died at six months from dysentery), I had a wonderful and uncomplicated childhood. We were certainly not rich in material possessions, but we were wealthy where it really counted. There was an abundance of love, hard work, loyalty, discipline, and laughter.

Dad had to quit school during the depression after the sixth-grade and Mom had only a high school education. As I look back, however, I still am amazed at both their knowledge and their wisdom. Their love for God and good was instilled in all of us in our growing years. They not only talked the talk, but walked the walk when it came to their Christianity.

I have read a myriad of books on the family. I have taken graduate level courses on the subject. I have counseled literally hundreds of households in crisis. I have taught family dynamics in the both the church and college environment. I openly confess, however, that the greatest and best principles for the home I know came from Ned and Hazel's classroom.

Even though both of them are gone now, I still start my morning prayers by thanking God for giving me such wonderful parents and such a special home. Perhaps distant memories seem more idyllic than they actually were, but the stories I share in the pages ahead are presented as accurately as I can recall them. You have to know this is true because I am certainly not the hero in any of them!

1.

Dying Where You Live

I remember the night "Ol' Man" Pence died in church. It happened during a revival service at our little country congregation in Quincy, Kentucky. We were standing, singing the old familiar hymn, "There Is Power in the Blood," when suddenly he went down, slumping in the pew. The worship service stopped and my dad and others tried to revive the precious old saint, but to no avail.

His visibly shaken daughter arrived with her husband a few moments later, but she soon calmed as she thought of the significance of it all. I heard her say, "There's no place my father would have rather been when he died."

Then there was Bert Cohen. He was a Jewish businessman in Ironton, Ohio, whose wife was a member of the Central Christian Church where I ministered for a number of years. He would sometimes attend services with her and so I often visited him in their home. Although well into his eighties, he loved playing golf. He went to the local country club several days a week and played a few holes with his friends. One day he told me, "I hope I die on the golf course." And he did. Putting out on Hole No. 1 at the Ironton Country Club one sunny afternoon, Mr. Cohen had a heart attack and died in the surroundings he loved.

Most folks in life are not so fortunate to be able to choose the place of their demise. Odds are, however, that we will probably die in circumstances and places indicative of where and how we lived.

I think of the young woman who was found dead on a frozen front lawn, early one wintry morning a number of years ago. Lying nearby was her critically injured husband. The night before they had been partying, something they did with great frequency it seems. Alcohol had turned their automobile into an unguided missile. Both had been thrown from the vehicle in the accident that had left the car a tangled heap of twisted metal. It was a tragic scene for someone to discover, but not one that really surprised those who knew the couple well.

If the Lord tarries, chances are you and I will also die like we have lived. I'm just wondering about it today, not trying to be offensive, but deadly serious nonetheless. What are the odds of you dying in church?

2.

The Best Template

It was one of those endless jobs that was never quite finished at the LeMaster house when I was growing up. Wallpapering! Every few months there was another room to do, it seemed, and Dad would call the troops together and we would get busy. Water was put on to boil and Argo starch was poured into the large pan to produce the paste we needed. No pre-glued paper existed back in those days! The kitchen table was cleared and Dad got out his square, edgers, rollers, and brushes to do the job right.

The ceiling had to be done first. I have often wondered since why anyone would paper their ceilings, but we did. Then we would tackle the walls. Each of us boys had a job: cutting, holding, pasting, or maybe just cleanup. We would attack the room with a vengeance, and within a few hours, the task was finished.

What I remember best was that Dad was always teaching while we were working. The papering lesson is one that especially has stayed with me. He would measure the first piece for the wall with expert precision and then use it as a template for the rest of the pieces to complete the job.

"No need to measure over if you cut the first piece right," he would say. "Just always remember to use that same piece every time for measuring the rest."

There was a certain redundancy to his lessons, but then you have to remember his pupils. We were little boys of ages six, eight, ten, or twelve. We needed to be told again and again and, with amazing patience, Dad did.

But little did my father realize that he was the best template for me! As I tackled the awesome task of trying to be a good father to my own children, I found myself often looking to his example. With a precision born of his Christian convictions, he measured out most of the steps I have followed in my own attempts at fatherhood.

Dad went home to be with the Lord over thirty years ago, but his influence upon my life remains strong. I know that I often seemed disinterested in the lessons he was trying to teach me, but they remain intact in my head and heart today, and will as long as I live.

It is a good reminder to all of us fathers. Dads, our shadows are long and leave a marked impression on our children, whether for good or evil. The Proverbs writer's admonition is well worth heeding, "Train a child in the way he should go, and when he is old he will not turn from it" (Proverbs 22:6).

3.

My Clothes!

Victoria Ryan tells a story with which I can identify. Her three year-old son was shown a portrait of his five older brothers, taken when they were much younger. He pointed and exclaimed, "Those guys are wearing my clothes!"

That is really the way it is when you grow up in a large family. I have four older brothers and an older sister, and a lot of my clothes were hand-me-downs. And if I was in the midst of a growth spurt, my younger brothers, Rowland, Joe, and Terry, would get a shot at the same outfits as well.

I never really paid much attention to it all until I hit those self-conscious years of early adolescence. Suddenly, I found myself embarrassed at the size of our family and the fact that we didn't always have new clothes to wear or steak to eat. It bugged me that we recycled jelly jars and turned them into drinking glasses. I hated it when some of my more well-to-do buddies would stop by our house. They could see our furniture was old and somewhat worn. How could it have been otherwise?

But somehow you finally grow up and your perspective changes. I look back wistfully to my childhood years now and realize how blessed I was. I had a father and mother who loved each other deeply and who shared that love with their nine children. They taught us about God and good and nearly smothered us with their care and concern.

No wonder my friends were always stopping by. There was more love and laughter in the LeMaster home than most of them could find anywhere else. I understand now why my folks ended up "adopting" so many of our friends who came to visit. They wouldn't leave! They found at our house what money couldn't buy.

I now know that one of the greatest blessings of my life was the family of my origin. There is no prouder moment for me today than when someone in my home community says to me, "You are one of Ned and Hazel's boys, aren't you?" Yes, I am!

4.

My Favorite Meal

I still remember it as the most delicious and satisfying meal of my life. I can't imagine anyone having a meal in this life that can measure up to it. I know I never will.

Please understand that although I am not a world-class connoisseur, I do have some knowledge about what is really good food. I have eaten pink salmon in the Space Needle Restaurant near the Pike Place Market in Seattle, Washington. Teresa and I have dined on delectable t-bone steaks in an abandoned mine converted into a restaurant in Kansas City, Missiouri, the Midwestern center for premium beef. I have eaten the best pizza in the world at our son-in-law's Christopher Pizza Company in downtown Nashville. He chose to close the business last year and I still crave his Bangkok Betty's oriental pie especially! I have even tried some of Bombay's finest cuisine in their International Airport restaurant.

To be honest, one only has to take a cursory look at my physique to know that I know something about good eating!

The best meal I ever had? Well, it was lentil soup and a bologna sandwich served to me by my mom one cold wintry afternoon several years ago. I was ministering in Huntington, West Virginia, at the time and was returning home after a long and tiring trip. Having been on the road all day, I was starved.

Mom, Dad, and I sat at the kitchen table in our old home place and visited for an hour or two. The lentil soup was hot and the warmth of the kitchen and the time with my parents made for the perfect meal. I have never had better!

Isn't it strange how the commonplace things of life often end up mattering to us most? We spend our time dreaming and planning for the exotic and the exciting, but when it is all said and done, it is the simple moments that live on in our hearts.

Perhaps it is the knowledge that I will never be able to share such a meal again in this life that makes it so much more special than any other. With my mother's recent death, both of my parents are now in glory with our Lord. I look forward to someday sharing with them in the great Marriage Feast of the Lamb, but until then I will cherish the memory of that wonderful afternoon.

5.

Blackberries

As I returned from a meeting in Louisville yesterday, I noticed a truck parked along the edge of the interstate and a man on the hillside picking blackberries. It brought back some vivid memories from my childhood days.

It always seemed to be the hottest days of the summer when my mother would send my brothers and me to pick blackberries. How I hated the job. To begin with, although it was 95 degrees in the shade, she would make us put on heavy jeans and long-sleeved shirts. Of course this was to protect us from the blackberry briars and the potential of chigger bites, but to a young boy of 8 or 9 it was seen as only a means of additional torture.

There was also the warning to watch for snakes. Mom only had to remind me once because I had absolutely no fondness for the critters. I don't believe I ever saw a snake while picking blackberries, but I became wall-eyed trying to keep one eye on the bushes and the other on the ground looking for them.

Then, there were the empty lard cans she gave us to fill to the brim before we returned. I don't know how much lard they held, but they seemed to be bottomless pits when it came to blackberries!

Like I say, I hated the job. But I found a way to not only endure it, but even to look forward to it. In my boyish little mind, I would think of a cold winter morning, waking up to another day of school. The smell of blackberries being heated on the stove would tickle my nose and send my taste buds into a frenzy. Have you ever eaten warm toast and butter smothered with hot blackberries poured over them? Ah, I can almost taste this delectable treat today!

Please don't think of am trying to trivialize the demanding nature of the Christian walk with this comparison, but I am convinced a difficult job becomes endurable when the ultimate goal is worthwhile. Truly, the Christian life is not easy. There's not a lot of instant gratification found in being a follower of Jesus Christ, especially in a godless society like ours. But heaven waits. And that, my friend, is a whole lot better than warm blackberries on a cold winter's morning!

6.

It Pays to Follow Instructions

Back in the mid-1960s, my family had a golf course near Quincy, KY. My oldest brother took an aunt's farm he had inherited and tried to turn it into Lea-Hi Greens Golf Club. It was a dream that wasn't well formulated or planned, but was still an interesting venture for the two years of its existence.

I worked almost full-time for two summers on the course, doing a little bit of everything. Our main hired worker was Jasper Dean Willis. "Japh" was an older, distant cousin whose major claim to fame was that he had once picked over one hundred quarts of strawberries in a day from our strawberry patch. I don't want to say that Japh was not an intelligent man, but I don't believe that NASA would have hired him—or me either!

In spite of all his other work, my dad supervised most of the jobs on the course. One day he asked Japh and me to build a trench around No. 5 green to allow water to drain from its hillside location.

I wasn't always the most willing worker, but for some reason I really got into this particular assignment. Starting early the next morning, Japh and I took mattocks and shovels and worked for hours, digging a ditch around the front side of the green. It was a hard job because the ground was clay-like, but by mid-afternoon we had the trench dug and the tile laid. We then covered it up with limestone rocks and stood back and admired our handiwork.

"Won't Dad be pleased," I thought to myself

He wasn't. Rather than digging the ditch above the green where we should have (and where he had indicated he wanted it), we had dug a useless trench of more than fifty feet in front of the green.

It pays to follow instructions, doesn't it? Japh and I had honestly worked hard and put our best efforts into the job, but the end result was worse than useless. Have you ever tried to untrench a trench?

Perhaps you feel like you are giving your best efforts in life and getting nowhere today. The problem may be much simpler than you realize. Have you been reading the instruction book? If so, are you following its directions?

7.

Grandma's Pickled Corn

It always seemed to be a risk worth taking. While Grandma Lowder and the others were preoccupied with more important things, I would sneak out to the backyard, pass the persimmon tree, and go down the dark stairs that led to the basement cellar. Lifting the wooden chuck that had long since replaced the Yale lock on the door, I would silently enter the cold, damp confines of the dirt-floored depository of Grandma's jams, preserves, canned beans, and pickled corn.

The pickled corn! Her other treasures were of no importance to me, but her pickled corn was too mouth-watering for a country boy to pass up. Like a thief executing the greatest heist of history, I would stealthily make my way through the darkness to the large brown-and-white crock that was covered with cheesecloth. Almost delicately pulling the cloth aside, I would reach down into the briny fluid to retrieve an ear of the delectable delight. Not daring to be caught, I would hide in the shadows of that cellar and consume my prize much too quickly, considering that most of us like to savor our culinary favorites.

I have searched the world over trying to find pickled corn that could begin to match Grandma's. Most of it is pickled in jars today and simply cannot compare with the briny ears that sat and soaked in old crocks in those damp, dark cellars of the past. Oh, I have the pleasure of eating a whole pickled ear of corn now and then; there are still some folks who like to do it the old-fashioned way. But even then, none tastes as good as hers.

I wonder what the difference was. Was it just a young boy's first experience with a taste that suited his palate? Was it the thrill of a "stolen pleasure," pickled corn enhanced by the adrenalin rush? Or, is it simply that my taste buds have acquiesced to time and lost their acuteness? I'm not sure, but there are days when I would give almost any monetary price to have that experience one more time.

And about my thievery. I certainly wasn't the first grandchild to do it, and I wouldn't be the last. Somehow, I sense that Grandma knew what we were up to anyway.

8.

The Disappearing Whipped Cream

It was the week before Thanksgiving in our eastern Kentucky home many, many years ago. School was out and there was an air of excitement as my brothers and I waited anxiously for the arrival of Thanksgiving Day. When I tell you it was a big day at our house, I really mean it. Relatives descended on us from everywhere, and if dinner was ever served for less than fifteen, I don't remember it.

How my brothers and I loved this time of the year! No school, a break from the humdrum routine, and finally something sweet in the house to eat!

You see, normally, there was nothing of consequence made from sugar in the LeMaster house. Mom had a thing about strong teeth and healthy bodies. No sweetened cereals, no soda pop, and certainly no chocolate candy. Can you imagine what a "sweet tooth" a little boy has when he is never allowed anything sweet to eat? But it was Thanksgiving and Mom had let the barriers down and pumpkin and mincemeat pies were being made—*and there was whipped cream in aerosol canisters hiding in the refrigerator*.

The big day finally arrived and Mom pulled the pumpkin pies from the oven just in time for dessert. She went to the refrigerator and got the two canisters of whipped cream, but to her complete surprise and embarrassment, nothing came out as she pressed the nozzle. Nothing! Both cans were empty, completely empty!

It remains one of the major mysteries of my childhood. What happened to the whipped cream? Mom knew my three younger brothers were too young and naive to be involved, but she sent an accusing glance toward my brother, Tony, and me. Tony and I looked at each other sheepishly, but kept our composure well enough to wonder aloud if the canisters were empty when Mom bought them.

The years have come and gone and Tony and I have never 'fessed up, but maybe it is time we did so. Operating independently, we were both guilty. The Bible says that stolen water is sweet, but I have a feeling the whipped cream would have tasted a lot better on the pumpkin pie!

9.

The American Patriot

He was thirty-three years old and had four little children at home when he received the notice in the mail. It wasn't the news he or his young wife wanted to hear. His draft number had come up and he was to report for induction into the United States Army. The year was 1944 and World War II had reached its zenith.

The hardships they would incur as a family over the next few years would lose their sting eventually, but it was difficult for her to think of holding things together while he was gone. The oldest child was only ten and the youngest one was in diapers.

Money was scarce. Somehow she got by on the $140 a month he received from the Army. Eventually another $15 a month would come as he was awarded the combat infantryman's badge for service under fire.

He would spend a year fighting with the Allied Forces in Italy. The thrill of seeing the Coliseum in Rome would be superseded by the vivid memory of the push across the Po River in one final battle. A part of the 10th Mountain Infantry, he knew that combat was near. He wrote to tell his wife that God had comforted him with the words of Psalm 118, verses 6 and 17, as he read his devotions prior to the conflict. There the Psalmist had written, "The Lord is on my side; I will not fear: what can man do unto me? I shall not die, but live, and declare the works of the Lord."

He did live and would finally return home like most soldiers, tired and sick and little shell-shocked. Every time the screen door slammed or a car backfired, he would almost jump out skin, his wife would later say. He tried to return to work immediately, but his employer sent him to the Veterans' Hospital instead, where he would spend over ninety days recovering from a service-induced lung infection.

He would never talk about his war experience much to his kids. They just knew that before the war he had been an avid hunter, but now his guns lay idle in their rack.

The price he paid was not the ultimate, of course. Some of his fellow soldiers would die and haunt his dreams. But the price was still high—economically, emotionally, and physically. However, to his dying day, if you would have asked him, he would have told you that he was glad to do his part for the country he loved. He was an American patriot and he was my dad.

Each Memorial Day we have the privilege of honoring those who have served in our Armed Forces and have been willing to die in order to insure our freedom. As a wonderfully blessed nation, we owe these brave patriots a great debt which we will never be able to properly repay. I am thankful we have a day set aside to pause and reflect upon their sacrifice.

10.

My Mother's Hands

It was mid-afternoon and I had nodded off to sleep on the couch while Mom dozed in her recliner nearby. We were alone, something really unusual considering the size of my family and the near constant stream of traffic at her house created by my siblings stopping by to check on her. My sister, Sue, had gone to visit her kids for a couple of days and my brother, Joe, who pinch hits willingly as mommy-sitter when needed, was getting out some cases that were due in his dental lab.

The total quiet must have awakened me. Mom was still asleep and I sat there, watching her. My gaze fell upon her hands, resting in her lap. Twisted from years of rheumatoid arthritis, every joint of almost every finger was swollen. The scars of time had left their indelible mark as well. Blood vessels beneath her thinning skin were broken, leaving the telltale purple blotches indicative of aging.

I found myself thinking of how a stranger might look at those hands and see them as unattractive or perhaps even call them grotesque or ugly. But I saw them through different eyes.

These were the hands that mopped my fevered brow when I was sick; wiped away my tears when I was hurt; held me close and tight when I was afraid; and, yes, wielded the rod of correction when it was needed.

These were the hands that labored day and night for decades cooking, cleaning, canning, clothing, and caring for the needs of a family almost large enough to qualify for its own separate zip code! They were the hands that labored on a shoe factory assembly line for eighteen years to help provide for our family's needs.

These were the hands that were clasped together in prayer beside the bed each night as she asked God for the strength to do a mother's job for one more day.

And, to me, they were the most beautiful hands in the world.

11.

Solanum Tuberosum

That is the scientific name of my favorite vegetable, the potato. Mash them, fry them, bake them, boil them, or scallop them. It doesn't really make much difference to me. I love to eat them. Period.

I have them on my mind today because it was just about this time of year that Dad would buy a couple of bushels of seed potatoes at the Vanceburg Farm Supply and try to persuade us that an eye-cutting party would be a lot of fun.

It was a communal affair and all of us got involved from an early age. I guess I am still surprised that my father trusted me to do it properly. Being left-handed and klutzy, the general rule at our house was that Phil was not allowed within ten feet of a knife or any potentially dangerous utensil. But because we raised such a large garden, all of us were pressed into action for this annual late March ritual.

We would gather in the kitchen, sitting in a circle. One by one we would take the seed potatoes and cut them into sections, each section having at least one good "eye." The eye, of course, was the sprout that, when properly planted, would produce numerous potatoes for harvesting in late summer.

With all of us pitching in, the job was quickly done and, a few days later, our potatoes became the first major crop in the ground for the new growing season. After several weeks, the potato plants were up and flourishing, giving promise of the potential tubers awaiting harvesting in late August or early September. Being the potato connoisseur that I am, it was always a comforting thing to see the hearty dark green plants blossoming with flowers beneath the summer sun.

But there were some disappointments. In each row there would be a gap or two where no potato plants would appear. Now, it was never because we had failed to properly space the seed potatoes in planting. Dad was way too meticulous a farmer for that. The problem was that sometimes the eye was not good. Planting a potato cube without a good eye was about as useful as planting a rock or a piece of cardboard!

The empty gaps in the rows mocked us. Potato eyes that are not really eyes have always disgusted me. I would like to call them hypocrites, but of course potatoes have no souls, do they?

With people it is another matter. When harvest time finally arrives, we will really know what God has always known about each one of us—how genuine our walk with Him has been.

12.

Haircut Day

Growing up in a household with seven brothers and a sister, I never had a "store bought" haircut during my childhood. Early on, Dad invested in a haircutting kit and became a pretty good barber by the time his eight boys had reached adulthood.

But how I hated haircutting day! There was a pecking order that demanded that my older brothers go first and that I had to wait for my inevitable shearing session. To complicate matters, my hair grows in an unusual pattern, similar to the vegetation of a Chia pet. Mike and Tony, two of my older brothers, had hair that was easy to cut and would lay obediently in place, but not mine. As a result, I believed Dad disliked cutting my hair almost as much as I disliked him doing it!

So as a little boy, I devised a method that I thought would save me from the whole process. When Dad would announce on a Saturday morning that it was haircutting day, I would go into hiding. My favorite spot was behind our genuine plastic Naugahyde couch in the living room. My theory was, with so many heads to cut, Dad would forget all about me and I would be spared (for at least another week). Falling asleep in my hiding place, I was able to dodge my rotation in the barber's chair.

But I was only prolonging the inevitable. I would end up as the last in line, having my hair cut after my three younger brothers. By then Dad was tired and more than a little aggravated with me for being less than a willing subject. As a result, my haircut would be his least professional effort of the day.

As my older brothers grew up and left home, I moved to the front of the line on haircutting day. Having reached adolescence, I had learned to appreciate the value of a good haircut and to look forward to the experience. I began to realize that this chore was no picnic for my father and that he was only trying to help me, not hurt me.

It is insightful how our perspective on things changes as we mature. The very things that we once dreaded, in time, can become the things we appreciate most. Funny, but I think I would give almost anything today to hear my dad say again, "Okay, boys, it's time to get your hair cut." Just to be able to climb up into the chair and spend a few minutes visiting with him would be worth almost any price.

13.

My Cousin's Tears

We whiled away the hours with aimless conversation, waiting for my father's open-heart surgery to be completed, Most of my siblings and I sat with my mother watching the elevator doors and hoping to see them open and the surgeons appear, bringing us the good news that all was well with Dad.

But that morning at Veterans' Hospital in Cleveland, Ohio, soon passed into afternoon, and the expected three-hour wait became six hours and then seven. As a young preacher, I knew that something was amiss, but I tried to convince myself that the surgery was delayed or some real emergency had called the doctors away before they could speak to us.

Finally, after eight hours, the elevator doors did open and two members of the surgical team stepped out. I tried to read their faces, but like consummate poker players they glanced at us but gave no clue as to the outcome. They motioned for us to go to a nearby conference room and it was then that my brother Ron asked what was on all of our minds, "He's dead, isn't he?" The chief surgeon's poker face failed and she launched into a practiced response, "The surgery went well, but when we took him off of the heart-lung bypass machine, a clot evidently went to his heart. We worked for over an hour trying to save him, but couldn't. I am sorry."

Her last sentences were unintelligible, muffled by the loud cries and wails coming from the family of this man who loved him deeply and leaned upon for strength and direction. Like my mom, my brothers and my sister, I gasped for breath, not able to comprehend how this seemingly indestructible man could possibly have died.

But it was true. At sixty-three years of age, Ned LeMaster, the strong patriarch of his family, had passed into eternity. Because of his committed relationship with Jesus Christ, we had no doubt about his destination, but we were brokenhearted nonetheless. For most of my family, it was the first death of great significance. We had lost grandparents, but they had lived long lives and their passing was expected. But Dad was still so young and vibrant and we needed him so much.

For me especially, his death seemed devastating. My father had always wanted one of his boys to become a preacher and I had fulfilled that dream. The last five years of his life found us growing closer and closer. I could always depend on Dad to solve my problems whether it was a washer and dryer that needed a hook-up or a theological question that needed an answer.

I was numb with grief and spent the next couple of days walking around like a robot, I am afraid. Perhaps mad at

God, I could take no comfort in His promises. Friends and members of the congregation where I served surrounded us with loving concern, but I was inconsolable.

The first visitation night at the funeral parlor arrived and hundreds of people filed by his open casket to express their sympathy. They reminded us of how significant his life had been. Their words were kind and well expressed, but my personal darkness was seemingly impenetrable.

But then my cousin, Keith, came up to the casket and looked down at my father's lifeless form. Keith and I were close in age and shared our growing up years. My parents and his spent much time together and our families loved each other. Keith stood there for a moment and never said a word. He looked at me and then I saw the tears streaming down his face.

For the first time since Dad's death, I felt a wave of comfort spread over me. Keith turned and walked away without a word, perhaps even a little embarrassed by his display of emotion. But I was touched and the healing started. I began to understand that others were hurting just like I was and that my father's life had impacted many people.

As a preacher who has officiated at over 600 funerals in my lifetime, people often ask me, "What do you say to the family of someone who has died?" Well, to this day I am not exactly sure of what the right words are, but I am convinced about the importance of being there and being willing to openly express your honest emotions. The apostle Paul was so right when he admonished us to "weep with those who weep" (Romans 12:15). Sometimes a tear is worth a thousand words.

14.

Yellow Bird

I sit in my home office on this mid-summer morning listening to Chris Isaak singing "Yellow Bird" from my computer music file. I downloaded the calypso classic recently because it reminds me so much of my mother who went home to be with the Lord less than two months ago.

Mom was ninety-four and in rapidly deteriorating health. Her mind, once so clear and sharp, had become clouded and confused. Her body, once so strong, was now so frail that we feared even our touch caused her discomfort or pain. It was time for her to go and our gracious Heavenly Father took her to be with Him and be reunited with Dad in glory.

I smile as I think of the song "Yellow Bird" and why it is a comfort to me now. Typically for me, lyrics often mean little. It is the music's melody that matters most. Thus this little island song, in spite of its melancholy words, resonates with my spirit because its melody makes me think of a happy event in my mother's life.

My brother, Ron, a very successful insurance agent, frequently received special travel bonuses for his sales acumen. He had won a trip to the Bahamas and invited my recently retired parents to go with him. In my mind, it was a trip of a lifetime for them. Mom would travel much after Dad's death, but this was the only major vacation outside of the states that they were able to share together.

From all accounts, they had a wonderful time in Bahamas. They were able to bask in the sun on the beach and just relax, something that neither of them had much of an opportunity to do before their retirement. Mom purchased a record album of music while there and played it constantly for weeks after their return. "Yellow Bird" was the song from the album that I remember best and love most for its poignant melody.

And today it comforts my heart to sit and listen to the song. It allows me to go back in my mind and recall a joyous time in my parents' lives. Thanks, Ron, for helping to make this particular memory a reality.

PART V—EXPERIENCES

In spite of the knowledge I was able to gain with my years of academic studies, I have learned, as you have, that the laboratory of life is the best teacher. For example, I had four years of study at a very good Bible college, but one year in a located ministry taught me so much more. I hear a lot of preachers who are reading this book saying very loudly, "Amen!"

Without getting credit for it, all of us are enrolled in CE classes that have the potential to add to our understanding about life every day that we live. Some of the lessons reinforce what we have previously learned, but many of them are totally new and help make life both exciting and challenging.

No doubt, the fact that I have been a preacher for four decades contributes to the effect that life experiences have on me. We preachers are constantly looking for illustrations for our sermons and have a tendency to turn anything that happens to us into one. There is not a family member or a friend of a preacher who is safe in this regard. If you are a part of my relational circle I want to publicly apologize, but also confess that I will probably do it again!

The articles in this section deal not only with incidents in my life, but my thoughts about public events, both current and past.

1.

A Small Change Can Make a Big Difference

Several years ago, I talked our Megan into visiting the Louisville Slugger Museum during a short trip to her new hometown. For the uninitiated, Louisville Slugger has been the premier producer of major league baseball bats since the turn of the last century. The Hillerich and Bradsby Company (parent company of Louisville Slugger), in the days before aluminum bats, made almost all of the wooden bats that boys of my generation used. Although 95 percent of bats today are metal, the Louisville Slugger factory continues to turn out 8,000 bats per week from the Northern Ash billets which arrive each Monday morning from a lumber mill in Pennsylvania.

Because the major leagues are the only "purists" still using wooden bats, they are the main customer (along with collectors) for this former booming business. Perhaps the most intriguing thing I learned in the tour of the factory was that almost all bats before 1935 weighed thirty-eight ounces or more. A thirty-eight ounce bat is heavy and close to what Babe Ruth used when he hit sixty homers for the Yankees back in 1927.

But it all began to change in 1935 when a brash young hitter made his first trip to Louisville and ordered bats weighing only thirty-two ounces. This kid had figured out something that had escaped the minds and calculations of all the major leaguers up until that time. He had determined that it was bat speed and not bat mass that was the most important variable in being able to hit a baseball long and true. Today most major leaguers use bats that weigh thirty-two ounces or less. Alex Rodriquez, the highest-paid player in baseball today, uses a thirty-one ounce bat that has a scoop of wood removed from its top, thus making it weigh in at just thirty ounces.

Every player in the major leagues who swings a bat for a living is indebted to the kid from 1935. He had the courage to challenge the prevailing paradigm and try something new. Maybe there's a lesson for us to learn from him as well. Sometimes a seemingly small change can make a big different whether it is in our personal lives or in the life of the church. It just takes the vision and courage to step out in faith with our Lord.

Oh, the kid from 1935? Why, Ted Williams, of course, perhaps the best pure hitter in the history of our national pastime!

2.

Tiger's Muff

I have been a sports' fan all of my life and, through the years, have watched my share of games, rounds, series, and tournaments on television. As I get older, however, I find myself watching less and less because most professional athletes seem to be overpaid prima donnas who very quickly grate on my nerves.

I do still watch the four major golf championships whenever I get the opportunity. I think I figured out the reason why as I watched Tiger Woods win his fourth green jacket at Augusta yesterday afternoon.

I love playing golf, even though in recent years the opportunities have become fewer and fewer because of my work schedule. At one time, I was a pretty decent player, but age and lack of play have turned me into a hacker. Unlike Tiger, I never take my "A" game to the course!

Anyway, back to my point. The courses for the four majors are always the toughest venues of the year for the pros, with narrow fairways, thick rough, and undulating greens that are concrete hard and almost impossible to hold. Because of the course difficulty, even the best players in the world end up looking amateurish from time to time.

I watched Tiger blow a shot on No. 10 yesterday. Camellia, as it is called, is traditionally the toughest hole on the course, a 495-yard, par 4. Just off the green, in the short rough in two, Woods got too much grass between his club and the ball and hit a pitch that traveled less than five feet, leaving him still short of the green. I thought to myself as I watched, "I could have done that!" Suddenly, watching the number one golfer in the world made me feel better about my own game.

Sometimes, I have to confess, I have had the same attitude in life. To make me feel better about my own lack of success, I have delighted in the *faux pas* of others. I have dismissed my own mistakes by pointing to my fellowman's failures.

Of course, such an attitude will never help me grow or do better in life, just as noting Tiger's infrequent failures have done nothing to improve by golf game. A much better plan would be to practice my swing and work on improving my walk with our Lord. Fore!

3.

Amazing Grace

Grace. Had any reminders of it lately? I have. Last week I was returning from my mother's late one evening, traveling the AA highway spur between Quincy and Grayson, Kentucky.

I wasn't really in a particular hurry, but there is something about that rather desolate stretch of road that seems to cause me to speed up. I came up behind a loaded semi-trailer truck that was starting up a long hill. I gunned the engine of my 1991 Lumina to get around it quickly, picking up even more speed in the process.

I saw the Kentucky State Highway Patrol vehicle's flashing lights almost immediately. Although he was going in the opposite direction, I had this strange feeling that he going to turn around and come after me. He did. Like a kid whose hand was caught in the cookie jar, I slowed down and headed for the side of the road. I pulled off the asphalt onto the graveled shoulder of the highway and came to a stop, awaiting my fate.

As he approached my car, I rolled down my window and heard him greet me rather kindly, saying, "Good evening, sir. How are you?"

It seemed like a strange question under the circumstances. But my reply, I suppose, of "just fine" was even stranger. I wasn't just fine. I was already trying to calculate in my mind what the monetary penalty was going to be and how many points it would mean against my driver's license.

"The reason I stopped you, sir, was that you were going seventy miles per hour and the speed limit is fifty-five. Could I see your driver's license and registration, please?"

The patrolman was so calm in his demeanor, much more so than I. I fumbled around, looking for my license in my billfold and checking the glove compartment for my registration. I handed him both with a less than steady hand, mumbling something about the slow truck.

"Don't I know you, sir?" he said next. "Where do you work?"

"In Grayson," I replied, not really wanting to confess what my occupation was.

"Oh?" he responded questioningly.

"Yes," I finally admitted. "I am the minister at the First Church of Christ there." I felt like I was confessing to being a serial killer, considering the reputation of preachers for having a "lead foot" when they get behind the steering wheel of an automobile.

"He's going to nail me for sure now," I thought to myself.

Then an amazing thing happened. He handed back my license and registration and said kindly, but firmly, "Mr. LeMaster, you need to slow down. Have a good evening."

And with that he was gone. No ticket, no warning, no strong reprimand. Just grace. Undeserved. Unmerited. But so sweet.

I slowed down.

4.

Reflections of an Old Man.

I appreciated the surprise fiftieth birthday party last night. It was so nice of you to remind me that this coming Friday I will have spent one-half of a century in this world. The many cards and gifts, both gag and good, touched my heart. Thanks!

For what it is worth, I would like to share some of the lessons I have learned along the way. After all, at fifty I am old enough to be a member of the AARP and would be considered a sage in some circles!

I have learned that people are wonderful if you think they are. Wherever I have been, folks have risen to reach my expectations of them. A long time ago I began believing in people, and I have never been sorry that I did. Not everyone rises to the challenge, but I have found that most do.

I have learned that if you put peanut butter and jelly on a piece of bread and accidentally drop it on the floor, it always lands jelly-side down. Always.

I have learned that if I have something bad or negative to say to someone, it is generally better for me to keep it to myself and not say it or write it. Once spoken or written, a word has a life of its own. You can't recall it or negate it, regardless of how hard you try.

I have learned that kids are the most honest people in the world. If a five year-old tells you that you are ugly, you probably are.

I have learned to practice grace with others. Since I am well aware of the grace that God has extended to me, I don't demand perfection from my peers. If someone stumbles and falls in my presence, I try to offer them my hand and not my boot. Eventually I know that I will need them to do the same for me.

I have learned that the speed of the cars in front of you on a busy highway is directly proportional to the amount of time you have to get to your destination. If you are in a hurry, they crawl. If you are on vacation and driving leisurely, they are all behind you playing Jeff Gordon and laying on the horn.

I have learned that God can be trusted. His timetable is not mine and His ways I don't always understand, but in the final analysis, He has never failed me. I can utterly and totally depend on Him.

I have learned that self-adhesives will stick to absolutely anything—except sometimes their intended surface.

I have learned that in life you generally get what you pay for. Invest in quality with your time and money and it will come back to you. Buy cheap or cheat on your investment of time and energy and the end result will reflect your attitude.

I have learned never to trust a golfer who pauses at the green and tries to recount his strokes for the hole.

I have learned that the first prayer I was introduced to as a child was also probably the most accurate. It began, 'God is great; God is good ...' And He is!

5.

School Daze

Over forty years ago, a cousin who was teaching in Cleveland, Ohio, at the time remarked about how unruly the high school students there had become. Her chief complaint? The boys refused to wear belts with their pants.

The recent rash of school violence reminds us once again how far we have slipped as a civilized nation in the past few decades. Hardly a semester passes today, it seems, without another incident of tragic proportions on a high school or middle school campus somewhere in America.

A friend of a friend resigned his teaching position a few years ago, saying, "I am tired of working in a system where the teacher is afraid of the principal, the principal is afraid of the superintendent, the superintendent is afraid of the school board, the school board is afraid of the parents, the parents are afraid of the kids, and the kids aren't afraid of anybody!"

Therein lies the problem in great part, I believe. The kids aren't afraid of anybody. Too many young people in America today grow up in homes where they are not taught to respect any authority. There is a hierarchy of respect that God intended for all of us to learn when we are young. It starts with a respect for Him. "The fear of the Lord is the beginning of wisdom," the Bible says (Proverbs 9:10). Building on this respect for God, children learn to respect the authority of their parents, governmental officials, and even their local school leaders.

The truth is that God is such a minor player in most American homes today that children grow up never knowing or understanding the importance of respecting authority. The end result is the murder and mayhem of Columbine, Pearl (MS), and Lancaster County (PA).

Moms and dads, don't try to excuse your responsibility by blaming the school system. Today's public school teacher has a job that is ten times harder than their predecessors of a generation ago. Most of them are doing the best they can with what you and I are giving them. In all honesty, the "product" teachers have to work with today is a difficult one. The new millennium's child is often rootless and thus sometimes ruthless. Until we begin to take God seriously again in the American home, I am afraid we can expect such carnage to continue.

6.

Superman Is Dead

The morning radio broadcast carried the sad news of the death of Christopher Reeve, who died yesterday of cardiac arrest at the age of fifty-two.

Reeve, who was selected for the role of Superman for the 1978 movie of that title, had been a quadriplegic since falling from his show horse in a 1995 accident. With courage and determination of heroic proportions, he had fought the battle for almost a decade to regain the use of his paralyzed limbs, always maintaining that one day he would walk again.

With athletic good looks and a 6'4" frame, Reeve was the perfect choice for the "man of steel" from the 200 aspirants who originally tried out for the part. He played the role well and became the epitome of the self-sufficient man until the tragedy that made him a mere shadow, physically speaking, of his former self.

Older baby boomers like me remember another Superman, George Reeves, who played the part on television in the 1950s. We grew up with the idea that there is indeed the possibility of being "faster than a speeding bullet and more powerful than a locomotive." The irony, of course, is that the first Superman died young as well. Depressed, evidently at being typecast and unable to find other roles, Reeves took his life in 1959 at the age of forty-three.

Perhaps there is a lesson in the Superman story for all of us. Modern man often thinks that he is limitless in his capabilities and is indeed self-sufficient. With the arrogance of William Henley, we announce to the world, "I am the master of my fate; I am the captain of my soul."

But then one day reality sets in and the truth becomes apparent. No man is superman. No man is completely self-sufficient. We all eventually must have help if we are going to make it in this life and in the world to come. We need a savior, not a superman. We need Jesus. I hope that Christopher Reeve realized this. I trust that you do as well.

7.

Shaking Trees

It's leaf-raking time for most folks in our community as the fall foliage has begun raining down in the past few days. I notice many of my neighbors busy with the task. I admire their work ethic, but I am personally inclined to a different mindset about fallen leaves. My theory is that you should wait until all of them are down, and then you should remind yourself that leaves are really compost and compost is good for the soil. Let fallen leaves lie!

I remember a young man in a community where I use to minister who was mentally handicapped. The joy of this special person's life was raking leaves in the fall. He couldn't wait for the hard frosts of late October or early November and the following rains to deposit the leaves on mother earth. Literally, he couldn't wait. He would begin shaking the tree limbs in order to hasten the process.

He did it because raking leaves was something he enjoyed doing. But consider his story in a different light with me. I think I know a number of people who are shaking trees, seemingly anxious for the leaves to fall. Unlike my young friend, these folks do it in dreaded anticipation, borrowing trouble from the future in the process.

Concerned about the well being of their loved ones, they shake the trees, worrying constantly about possible sickness, accidents and pending tragedies. Or, anxious about the economy, they shake the trees, watching the Dow Jones daily with racing hearts and troubled minds. Or, frightened by a modern world filled with terroristic threats, they shake the trees and die a thousand deaths.

Please understand that I realize we must be mindful of such concerns, but I am convinced that our Heavenly Father does not want us to spend our time worrying about unfallen leaves. Jesus said in the Sermon on the Mount, "Do not worry about tomorrow, for tomorrow will worry about itself. Each day has enough trouble of its own" (Matthew 6:34).

Our Lord's command is sound advice for leaf rakers, tree shakers, and anybody else. There is no need for us to shake the trees, my friend; the Tree Maker will take care of us if we will trust in Him.

8.

Trophies in the Attic

While cleaning out the attic recently, I came across a box filled with basketball trophies from my high school and college days. I was surprised to see how tarnished and broken they had become with the passing years. Once tall soldiers holding miniature basketballs aloft in outstretched arms, now most of the figures have been broken off at their bases. The shiny gold and silver gloss of the awards has dulled and an ugly patina with some rust spots has started to appear on most of them.

What a metaphor of life, I thought to myself. Here I was thirty-plus years later, carefully working at a task that demanded that I protect my fragile back and gimpy knees. I couldn't help but find my mind wandering back to an earlier day when I had raced up and down the basketball court with reckless abandon, giving little thought or worry to bodily concerns. In those days, I literally threw myself into the fray, diving for loose basketballs and running into thinly-padded brick walls. Now, quite gingerly, I went about a much less demanding task, worrying if I would be able to get out of bed the next morning.

Even more, though, I found myself thinking of how quickly the years from youth to middle age have passed. It seems like only yesterday that I was a kid bouncing a basketball down the floor at the old Prichard gym, listening as Coach Dace and Mr. G called out instructions. Now I anxiously await each month's arrival of AARP's newsletter. I need that information!

What's the point? Simply this. Life is short regardless of how many years God blesses us with in this world. This is why it is absolutely imperative that we seize each day and live it to the fullest for Him. Have you been thinking about doing some good deed? Ending some bad habit? Telling someone you love about Jesus? Do it today!

9.

Heavenly Real Estate

Real estate advertisements always intrigue me. It is not just what they are selling, but how they go about it. There are several standard phrases that are used to indicate that a particular property is special. One of my favorites is: *"Must be seen to be appreciated."*

I think I know what they mean when they list a property and use that phrase. They are saying, "This piece of property is much nicer than we can describe simply by using words—or even pictures." Having looked at a lot of real estate in the past couple of years, I need to tell you that this advertising come-on is usually hyperbole, if not a total misrepresentation!

The apostle John, however, seems to be conveying this very thought to us in the book of Revelation with no exaggeration. With figures, symbols, visions, and apocalyptic language, he reveals a future world that leaves us begging for more precise verbiage as to its beauty and wonder.

In his description of heaven, John talks about walls of jasper, gates of pearl and streets of gold. The city is so beautiful that the only measuring rod which seems adequate is one made of gold itself. There is no need of sun or moon because the Lord Jesus, the precious Lamb of God, is the light.

It is almost as if John is grasping for words that can, in some way, describe what he is seeing. The old hymn we use to sing perhaps says it best, "The half has not been fancied this side the golden shore!"

No hyperbole or attempt to oversell here. I am convinced that heaven *"must be seen to be appreciated."* I find myself thinking of my loved ones who have gone to be with the Lord and I realize that they must be thinking the same thought. Their first moment in heaven they were probably saying, "Wow, if only they knew back on earth what a wonderful place this is! If only I could tell them how beautiful and glorious heaven is. If only they knew how much joy and happiness I am finding here!"

The next time you start wondering and worrying about someone you love who has gone home to heaven, just remember the real estate ad, *"Must be seen to be appreciated!"* Comfort yourself with the thought that your loved ones are indeed in a far better place. Commit yourself once again to joining them when this life is over.

10.

The Real Proof of the Unisex Fallacy

I never really believed much in the unisex movement that began a generation ago. After all, the Bible says "male and female created he them" (Genesis 1:27). But just in case you still wonder about it all, I have a sure-fire way of proving to you that there is a world of difference between the sexes. Just go shopping with a woman for a day.

A woman will travel a dozen miles and spend an extra $5 on gasoline to save thirty-five cents on a bottle of ketchup and feel good about the experience. A man will grab a jar of Del Monte's off the shelf and never look at the price. He just knows that it is the ketchup that pours slower and that's endorsed by Michael Jordan.

A woman will spend an hour of her time (she's paid $15 per hour at work) to clip coupons which will save her $5 at the grocery store. Most men have never willingly used a coupon in their entire lives.

A woman will buy ten cans of gnu meat because it is on sale ten for $3.95, although none of her family really likes it and she probably won't use ten cans of it during the next millennium. Why? It's on sale, you silly thing!

If it is true that a woman has a gene for bargain hunting, it is also true that she has another for comparison shopping. A woman will go into a store and find an item which she likes. She will try it on and find that it fits perfectly and looks great on her. Does she buy it? Certainly not! You know better than that! The task is not finished until she has gone to at least a dozen other stores searching for the same or a similar item at a better price. Six exhausting hours later she returns to the first store and the first item and makes her purchase. Her husband is exasperated, but she has only done what any normal woman would do.

A man, by comparison, will walk into an automobile show room and purchase a $30,000 truck in less than ten minutes. As long as it is not pink and has a V-8 engine and a gun rack behind the seat, he's satisfied.

I noticed something else different about women in this regard. When they get home at the end of a shopping day, they have to show off their purchases to every other woman in a mile radius, sort of like a fisherman displaying the catch of the day. I could go on, but I think you have the point.

No, you will never convince me that women are even remotely the same as men. I've shopped with too many of them to ever be fooled again.

11.

What's on My Silver Shelf?

One of the blessings of being a minister is that people are constantly passing along written items that they think will be useful to you. As a result, I have literally hundreds of poems, jokes, articles, and prose pieces on a myriad of subjects in my files

Betty Ramey gave me a copy of an Emily Dickinson poem that I treasure. Dickinson was something of an enigma in life, publishing only ten of her more than 2,000 poems. It would be left to friends to popularize her work after her death. Today she is considered by many to be the greatest female writer of verse in our country's history.

This particular short poem is on values and reads:

It dropped so low in my regard

I heard it hit the ground,

And go to pieces on the stones

At the bottom of my mind;

Yet blamed the fate that fractured, less

Than I reviled myself

For entertaining plated wares

Upon my silver shelf.[2]

One has to wonder what it was in Dickinson's life that she once thought so important only to find later that she had grossly overvalued it.

I have no clue in that regard, but I am well aware of many things in my life that once assumed center stage that now seem of only token importance. As a young boy growing up, I was consumed with a love for sports. If it was a ball and you could bounce it, throw it, kick it, or catch it, I was interested. In retrospect, how much precious time I wasted on those particular "plated wares" that I had placed upon my silver shelf.

With God's help, I hope I have learned to be much more focused on the things that are really important today. Life is too short to waste on trivial pursuits. Our silver shelves demand something better.

12.

A Job Worth Doing

Sometimes when I am working in our yard, I find myself thinking about deep theological issues. That may surprise you, but really what else is a preacher supposed to do when he is involved in such a mundane task? Recently as I was mowing and raking and weeding, I began pondering the question: "What kind of tents did the apostle Paul make?"

You will remember that in order to support his ministry, Paul was a tent-maker. He shared in that trade from time to time with his two close friends, Aquila and Priscilla. It was a common and essential occupation of the first century world.

As I huffed and puffed my way through my time-consuming, boring job, I thought of Paul and wondered as to his attitude about his tent-making. Did he enjoy it? I doubt it. He had more important things to do. As a Christian missionary, his mandate was to reach the unreached of the world for Jesus Christ. Tent-making, in one sense, stood in the way. Every stitch he sewed must have reminded him that on the road to Damascus he had received a call that was far more exciting and challenging.

But what kind of tents did he make? Now, I am not talking about brand names here or styles. I am talking about quality. Was Paul a good tent-maker? Was his workmanship first-class? Did people get their money's worth when they went to Paul's Tent Works, Unincorporated, for a new canvas?

I know the answer that the question. Paul's tents were the best! They had to be. He who had instructed others, saying, *"Whatever you do, work at it with all your heart, as working for the Lord, not for men,"* (Colossians 3:23) would not have been satisfied with less from himself.

Thinking about it made me do a better job on the lawn-mowing. Really! Think of it! Long before our parents and teachers and employers said it, Paul said it. <u>A job worth doing is worth doing well</u>!

13.

A Ton or an Ounce

He was known as the "poet laureate of childhood" because of his many poems written for young people, but most folks today have probably never heard of him. He certainly doesn't rank with Wordsworth or Longfellow or any the other great poets of our country's history. Nonetheless, he is still a favorite of mine.

His name was Edmund Vance Cooke and he endeared himself to me with a poem I first encountered during my undergraduate days at Kentucky Christian University. It wasn't an assigned reading for any of my literature classes;

I discovered it when I bought a volume in the school bookstore entitled *One Hundred and One Famous Poems*. I am sure I purchased the book with the intention of using some of the poems in my sermons. No doubt I have. But the serendipity in buying the book was the finding of Cooke's poem, "How Did You Die?"

A consummate worrier as a young man, I found that Cooke's poem spoke to my heart about the importance of putting things into perspective and understanding that problems in life are only as large as we let them become in our minds and hearts.

My favorite stanza of the poem says it best,

Oh, a trouble's a ton, or a trouble's an ounce,

Or a trouble is what you make it.

And it isn't the fact that you're hurt that counts,

But only how did you take it.[3]

For years, even as a young man, I had been practicing turning lightweight troubles into heavyweight problems. Cooke's poem reinforced in me the biblical mandate of

Philippians 4:6, "Do not be anxious about anything, but in everything, by prayer and petition, with thanksgiving, present your requests to God."

Cooke was right. We can choose to allow our problems to be molehills or mountains. It is up to us. The next time you are starting to stew over some issue, think of the poet's words. There is a great difference in an ounce and a ton!

14.

Loser's Limp

Our half-Samoyed dog, Prissy, has almost healed from her recent rendezvous with a pickup truck in front of our house. No broken bones, the vet said, only a leg that had been scraped to the bone on the highway asphalt.

As I said, the healing process is almost complete, but I am afraid that Prissy will always have a "loser's limp" to remind her of that fateful Saturday afternoon.

To be honest, I am really glad about it all. Prissy has been very reluctant to cross the street since her mishap and shows no desire whatsoever to visit her doggy friends south of West

Main. I believe that her limp reminds her of her accident and is probably helping to prevent a reoccurrence.

Loser's limp, however, does not seem to be such a positive blessing in the spiritual realm. You know what I am talking about. A failed marriage, a financial indiscretion, a job loss, flunking out of college. The list could go on *ad nauseum* of those things which knock us off our feet and start us hobbling.

The truth is that almost all of us could give some reason for "limping" through life. Rare indeed is the person who manages to miss all the pitfalls on the road to glory. Frankly, in my many years of located ministry, I have yet to meet such a person.

The apostle Paul was someone who could have developed a major league loser's limp if he so desired. As a persecutor of the Church, he had held the coats of those who stoned the first Christian martyr, Stephen. He could honestly refer to himself as "chief of sinners" (I Timothy 1:15, KJV).

But he did not allow his past to slow him down in his desire to serve Jesus Christ. His zeal never flagged in his efforts to share the Good News once he found it. Perhaps his words from Philippians 3:13, 14, say it best, "Forgetting what is behind...I press on toward the goal to win the prize for which God has called me." Maybe we need to memorize Paul's words and hide them in our hearts for those days when our limp becomes real noticeable. If God has forgiven and forgotten our past, we should, too!

PART VI—CHURCH

From the world's perspective, I have been a full-time employee of the church since September of 1970 when Teresa and I moved into the parsonage of the First Christian Church in Mt. Olivet, Kentucky. If you add my three years of weekend ministry during my student days at Kentucky Christian College to those thirty-nine years, then I have spent well over two-thirds of my life working with the church.

As a senior minister for almost all of those years, I have been charged by the local congregational leadership with the responsibility of casting the vision and encouraging the membership to be the Church in the best possible sense of the word.

Please understand that I understand how the world tends to look at the church in the twenty-first century. I would remiss if I did not admit that there are times when I, too, become disgruntled and wearied by the less-than-perfect people who comprise the body of Christ. Nonetheless, I believe the Church is the God-ordained organism that continues to change lives and the world for good today, just as it has for the past two thousand years. As one of its imperfect parts, I openly confess that I love the Church!

The articles in this section come from my experiences in the church environment. I have also included observational and inspirational pieces that seemed best suited for this particular category.

1.

Mt. Olivet

Almost thirty years to the day, I am scheduled to speak again to the graduating class of Mt. Olivet Deming High School this week. Virgil and Sue Messer's nephew, Tommy, is an outstanding member of that class and had the opportunity to pick the speaker. I feel honored to be his selection.

My mind is flooded with memories today as I anticipate our visit. What a special place Mt. Olivet, Kentucky, has in Teresa and my hearts!

It was in the fall of 1970 that we began our three years of ministry there. I was twenty-two and Teresa was only twenty. Even after four years of Bible college and two years of weekend preaching, what I knew about ministry could have fitted into a thimble with room to spare. I was such a poor speaker that it actually took three "trial" sermons before they agreed to call us as their parsonage family.

Mt. Olivet is the county seat of the smallest county in the state of Kentucky. The last census indicates that Robertson County still has just a little over 2,000 residents. The county's only real claim to fame is that people there live longer than anywhere else in the state. Among our neighbors when we moved into the parsonage on Main Street were Judge Paynter who was ninety, Claudia Wells who was eighty-eight, and Mrs. Smith who was eighty-five years old. One church member, R. T. Baker, would celebrate his 101st birthday during our tenure.

A preacher's first ministry is crucial. It can either make him or break him. I've seen the "breaking option" with far too many of my colleagues to even try to calculate the percentages. After a couple of terrifying years in the wrong place or with the wrong people, they are ready to sell insurance, dig ditches, or do anything but work in the church.

But Mt. Olivet was a dream come true for Teresa and me. The wonderful people there took us under their wings and loved us. Patiently, they nursed us through our mistakes and taught us what we needed to know. We would go to our next ministry with confidence and the sense that God could and would use us.

There's a debt we owe to the folks of that special little community that we will never be able to repay. I look forward, at least, to making an installment on this debt this coming Friday evening.

2.

Let Me Have Christmas

Every December we revisit the issue of whether Christians have a right to publicly and freely express their joy at the coming of the Messiah, Jesus Christ. For several decades now, the politically-correct crowd has suggested that we tone it down especially in any public display. No Christmas carols in department stores, no nativity scenes on community property, and not even any greetings of "Merry Christmas" to people we meet on the street.

I disagree! Let me explain my viewpoint by relating a story from my ministerial past.

It was one of the most unusual funerals I ever conducted. The deceased woman had converted to Judaism when she married her Jewish husband. He had long since died, and as she grew older, she had a strong desire to return to the Christian faith of her youth. And she did. I took her confession in a hospital room and we cried together tears of joy.

But her family connections were now strongly Jewish and I was asked to share the funeral with a young rabbi. He called me and very bluntly said, "You know, if you mention Jesus at the memorial service you will offend the Jewish people present."

Could I just do my eulogy and leave Jesus out? Of course, I replied that what he was asking of me was impossible. I couldn't preach a sermon, I couldn't offer a eulogy, I couldn't even pray a prayer without mentioning Jesus!

To be honest, I was much more worried about offending God by not talking about His Son than offending anyone else. To make a long story short, we compromised. I preached the funeral (and talked about Jesus) and the rabbi did the graveside service (and talked about death).

I have a few words for the ACLU, the Jewish community, the Muslim community, the public school administrators, and anyone else up in arms about the Christian emphasis at Christmas time: we Christians have feelings and rights, too! I find myself totally offended when you suggest I can't talk about Jesus or put on display the symbols representing His birth at this season of the year.

When my religious freedom and yours clash in this country, it would seem that compromise is in order. I will make you a deal. If you will let me rejoice and celebrate Christ's birth at Christmas, I won't say a word about your overt acts of religiosity on Hanukkah, Ramadan, or Wesak.

Go ahead. Light a candle. Take a pilgrimage. Chant a mantra. Put up a Star of David or erect a statue of Buddha. It's a free country. But in the name of fairness, let me have Christmas.

3.

Leaving Jesus Out

The voice on the other end of the phone line sounded almost frantic. A man I had met in a summer church softball league needed to talk to someone. Would I mind if he stopped by my office?

When he arrived a short time later, he told me a disjointed, rambling story of a life that had once been seemingly stable, but now had become chaotic. Six years before, he explained, he had shot and killed his wife in a fit of rage. Convicted of manslaughter, he had spent several years in prison, but early parole had brought him his freedom once more.

His presenting problem concerned his young daughter whom he had not seen in those six years. His wife's parents had gotten custody of her after the shooting and had refused to let him have any contact with her whatsoever.

In great anguish he told me how he often imagined walking down the streets of our city, Huntington, West Virginia, and passing his little girl without being able to recognize her. His heart was breaking because he still had a father's love for his daughter and could not bear the thought of spending the rest of his life without her.

There was no counseling magic I could apply to the problem. In fact, to this day I cannot tell you the outcome of the story. Not even knowing his full name or where he lived, follow up was impossible. When he left my office that day, I never saw him again.

What stays in my mind, however, are the first words he spoke to me when he walked through the office door that afternoon. With arms gesturing, he said, "Now, preacher, let's just leave Jesus out of this, okay?"

How could I tell him that was the whole problem? The consequences of his present life were a result of his decision to leave Jesus out.

There are far too many people in our world who want to leave Jesus out and still hope for a happy existence. It just won't work. Not for that man, not for you or me or anyone else. Leaving Jesus out of life's equation is the surest route to failure that I know.

While on earth, He said, "I am the way, the truth and the life. No man comes to the Father except through me" (John 14:6). I am convinced that His words are true. The only sure path to the abundant life here and in eternity is through Jesus Christ. My message to the world, with all the earnestness I can muster, is simply this, "Let Jesus in!"

4.

Eternity

The thoroughbreds raced playfully across the immaculate fields of the Paris, Kentucky, horse farms. It was a beautiful early fall day in the central part of the Bluegrass state; the air was crisp and the sky was a cloudless blue. The neat and tidy homes of that Bourbon County community were as impressive as their adjacent horse farms. There are few drives in America that are as beautiful, in my estimation, as traveling the Paris Pike to Lexington.

As a young preacher, I fell in love with the area and found myself drinking in every picture, every scene as I traveled the fifty-some miles for the first time that autumn of 1970. It would be a trip I would repeat scores of times in our three and one-half years of ministry in the little town of Mt. Olivet.

Believe it or not, the most impressive part of the journey for me was the cemetery that lay off to the right as you leave Paris. Immaculately groomed like the rest of the area, there was a large whitened archway that led into the cemetery. Wrought iron fences extended from the archway on either side, meaning that everyone who came there had to pass through it.

The archway contained a simple message on its exterior that everyone would see as they entered. The words were from Hebrews 9:27 (KJV). You probably know them: "It is appointed unto man once to die, but after this the judgment."

Appropriate words for a cemetery entrance. And an appropriate reminder for all of us who travel life's highway. There is a destination at the end of this journey. In spite of what the atheist would say, we came from somewhere and we are going to somewhere.

It is a glorious thought or a horrendous thought, depending upon your destination, isn't it? Eternity awaits each of us. What preparations are we making for this inevitable final chapter of our lives?

5.

A Summer Silent Night

It was 93°F outside yesterday afternoon, which made the special music for the International Ministry service here at First Church of Christ seem rather bizarre. HeeKap Lee's nephew, June, stood before the entire congregation and sang *Silent Night*. No, it was not a joke, and its significance was greater than most people attending probably realized.

June and his younger sister, Jasmine, had been visiting with the Lees for the past month along with a couple of Yoon Lee's family members from South Korea. The purpose of the trip was to learn English better and to gain insight into our American culture.

June and Jasmine are children of HeeKap's oldest brother who is a very wealthy man and a devout Buddhist. In South Korea, the family hierarchy is much more rigid and precise than in most countries. The "pecking order" dictates that the eldest son is the most respected and honored and that youngest son is considered almost a nonentity. HeeKap is the youngest son.

To say that HeeKap's brother has never understood or appreciated his youngest sibling's Christianity would be an extreme understatement. With great contempt, he has discounted his little brother's faith and lack of zeal for pursuing the capitalistic dream. He sent his children to visit HeeKap with strict orders not to go to church or be fooled by the Christian lifestyle.

June spent his first few days in America following his father's directives and looking at HeeKap and Yoon's faith with a jaundiced eye. But then something happened. Some of you spent afternoons speaking English and sharing American culture with him. He attended church services. He spent a week at Lake James Missions' School. Many Christians prayed for him and his sister at the Lees' urging.

June's heart began to soften and finally, with great humility, he apologized to HeeKap for his negative attitude. Then came his interesting request, "Could I sing the only Christian song I know at the worship service to express my appreciation for you and the kindness of the Christian people?"

So June sang *Silent Night* on a summer afternoon and, in the same service, Jasmine was baptized into Christ. As they fly back to South Korea today, the final chapter of the story is yet to be written, but June returns home with a changed mind and an open heart.

I hope that you will join me in praying for June and Jasmine and for their father. And, thank you, because in some small way, you may have made a difference in a young South Korean man's eternity.

6.

The Rich Little Boys of Mozambique

It was the summer of 1999 and I had traveled to Africa to visit some of our missionaries in Zimbabwe. A few days later, I went by truck with a friend and two missionaries to neighboring Mozambique where the mission was trying to start some churches.

At that time, Mozambique was a war-torn nation that had suffered through 15 years of civil conflict and fighting. Crossing the border into the town of Chichulachula was not really a difficult task. The tariff was only 83 Zim dollars, a little over $5 American. The bad news was that we learned from the border patrol that it would cost us $30 American to cross back into Zimbabwe at the end of our visit. The border patrol went on to tell us that they would not accept Zim dollars, Mozambique medicais, or even American Express travelers' checks! My problem was that I had brought only travelers' checks and an American $100 bill.

We decided to enter Mozambique anyway, hoping that we could somehow find change for my $100. We tried the bank in this little town of 10,000 refugees, but they only had medicais. The bank did give us the name of a local man who might be able to help. With the assistance of one of the villagers, we were taken to this man's rather elaborate compound. Amazingly, without quibbling or questioning, he willingly gave me two twenties, a ten, and a fifty dollar bill in exchange for my hundred. No fee, no charge. What a relief! I saw the easy exchange then as a "God thing," and I still do today.

I tell you that story to tell you another story. While we were surveying the town, we were followed everywhere by a group of little boys who obviously had suffered the devastation of war. Their clothes were ill-fitting and tattered, their feet were shoeless, and their faces dirty. But laughing and kicking a soccer ball made of plastic bags and string, they followed us throughout the dusty streets with faces aglow with what I could only call joy. With holes in their pants, I am sure that not a one of them had a single penny or even a centavo (100th of a medicai). But for them it was a great day. The brilliant African sun was shining; they were alive and living in the moment.

Much more than me. Worried over my $70 problem (if I had to surrender my $100 back at the Zimbabwean border), I had been so preoccupied with my money woes that I had failed to take in the amazing sights and sounds of my only foray into Mozambique. We visited the marketplace and interacted with dozens of people, but most of it was lost on me. I was too busy worrying.

I will leave the application to you, my friend. I am far too embarrassed by the story to even consider it. I can only say I know who the real pauper was that day.

7.

No Coincidences

It was 3 a.m., and there I was in the Bombay (Mumbai) national airport cradling an Indian baby in my arms. The scene may sound strange to you, but I was not really surprised. It was an obvious answer to prayer.

The story began a few weeks before when I had made the commitment to go to Kerala, a state in southwest India, to teach at a Bible college there and preach evangelistic services. It was my first time to travel internationally and I was making the trip alone. My fears were heightened by warnings about the Bombay airports. Landing at the international airport, I would have to go to the national airport to catch a plane to Trivandrum, the capital city of Kerala.

"You will run into all kinds of people, beggars and thieves included, and really will need someone to help you make the transfer," I had been told. Well, there was no one who could make the trip with me, and I was determined to go. Thus I prayed a very specific prayer.

"God, please provide someone for me at the Bombay national airport that understands English and will help me get safely to my destination."

And in an amazing fashion He did! I arrived by taxi at the airport and almost immediately ran into a couple returning to their native Kerala from their home in London. That's right, London! The husband spoke with a British accent, using words like "bloke" and "quid." Never a fan of the true English dialect, on this occasion, it sounded like music to my ears.

The couple had two young children and was travel-weary just like me. We sat through the night talking, unable to sleep. From time to time I would take their little baby in my arms, to rest Mom and Dad from the chore.

The young father had traveled enough internationally to explain in detail what I needed to do to make my next connection. And that was enough. With each succeeding transfer, God provided individuals, out of nowhere seemingly, to translate for me and help me reach my next stop.

Now some people would probably call it luck or coincidence, but I know better. It was answered prayer. The incident went into *My Catalog of Answered Prayers* which I have developed over the years. *My Catalog of Answered Prayers* is a book in my heart, not on paper. It grows in volume with almost each passing day. I love to peruse its pages and remind myself of a loving Father who really wants to bless His children's lives.

8.

Helping Your Neighbor

It is one of those scenes that has left an indelible mark on my memory. From time to time it graces my conscious mind and always makes me smile.

It took place during my years of serving as dean for Junior Week at Howell's Mill Christian Assembly. Teresa and I shared this responsibility for a dozen summers at the Ona, West Virginia, camp back in the days when we were younger and just a little more energetic.

In order to make survival of such an intensive experience possible for all people involved, we divided the campers up into teams. Each team would consist of about twelve to fifteen young people, ages nine to eleven. The teams would eat together, work on projects together, and participate in sport activities as units.

Jeff and Charley were the "Mutt and Jeff" of one team that particular year. Jeff was at the top of the age range and growing quickly into a young adult. He stood several inches taller than anyone else on his team. Charley was at the other end of the spectrum. The growth spurt hadn't started for the little fellow and probably never would. He was shorter than almost all of the girls in camp.

"Camp Olympics Day" arrived on Thursday and the teams were competing in a race that required all team members to participate. The first team to get <u>all of their members</u> across the finish line would win.

On your mark, get set, go! Jeff was at the finish line almost before some of the kids got started. Running dead last, going as fast as his short legs would carry him, was

Charley! If he finished last, his team would lose and Charley would be blamed for letting them down.

But then, out of the blue, Jeff did an amazing thing. Running back toward the starting line, he intercepted Charley, picked him up and carried him across the finish line ahead of several other runners! It was an unorthodox move, but counted as far as the judges were concerned. Instead of being a scapegoat, Charley was able to join Jeff and his teammates in the winner's circle.

Jeff reinforced an important lesson for all of us that day. While most of us stood by, amused or indifferent to Charley's predicament, he got busy helping his little friend.

There are times in life when all of us find ourselves in Charley's shoes. We have fallen behind and simply cannot make it without help. What a blessing it is when someone like Jeff comes along! The apostle Paul reminds us in Galatians 6:2, "Carry each other's burdens, and in this way you will fulfill the law of Christ."

9.

Casting a Vote against a Familiar Foe

The immutable truths of God's Word are unchanging and much be faithfully followed if we are going to be the Church. Clinging to tradition, however, has kept more congregations from accomplishing God's Will than anything else I have experienced in four decades of ministry. The early Church was a vibrant, growing organism, and God intends for her to be so today. In order to accomplish this growth, change is absolutely essential.

Whenever we vote for positive change in the local congregation, we are also casting a vote against another personality who most of us know well. We became acquainted with him early on in life, and he has hung around throughout the years. He has an agenda and it is a familiar one. It includes the following items:

1. Resist change at any cost. Everybody knows that the tried and true is always better. New programs and new ideas demand far too much energy and money.

2. Always choose maintenance over growth. Growth is scary and messy and calls for increased effort and additional resources. The battle cry of the wise organization is "Maintain!"

3. Stay away from the cutting edge, you may get hurt. Avoid new concepts and methodologies like the plague! It is much better to be staid and boring than to risk failure by trying something revolutionary.

4. Memorize the phrase: *"We have never done it that way before."* This statement will go a long way towards discouraging those malcontents who are always advocating change and growth. Repeat if often—and with feeling.

5. Learn to put a negative spin on any positive progress. Never contribute anything to the hand of God when you can explain it away by luck or circumstance.

6. Reserve the right to say, "I told you so," when new projects or programs stumble.

Who is this familiar figure with his well-defined agenda? Why, Mr. Status Quo, of course! When we vote for change, we send a strong message to him. The message is, "Your days of running and ruling the church are over. Start packing! You're not welcome here anymore."

10.

Something Happened Here

Teresa and I were in Lexington on Saturday and stopped for lunch at Joe Bologna's, one of our favorite places to eat. It was a beautiful afternoon, and we spent part of it just walking around the historic section of Lexington that surrounds the restaurant.

Many of the houses there have plaques on them, indicating who lived there and what happened there generations ago. As we walked down Maxwell Street, we came upon an old house that had such a marker by its front door. I had to chuckle when I read it. It read: IN THE YEAR 1897 NOTHING HAPPENED HERE.

I found myself thinking of what someone had said of our church here in Grayson recently. They had remarked that there were far too many things going on at our building, far too many groups and too many people using the church for too many activities.

I wasn't offended by their words. In fact, I took the criticism as an indication that perhaps we are moving in the right direction. My vision of a church that is pleasing to the Lord is a vision of one that is a constant hub of positive activity for God and good.

Sure, I want our building to look nice, but I am not upset that the carpets get dirty and there are smudge marks on the walls from time to time. I am not disappointed that sometimes in the middle of the week there is so much noise outside my office that I can hardly think; kids laughing, teenagers practicing music, people talking.

I want our church building to be a happening place, a place where people can feel at home, an inviting place. Whatever we can do to make this a reality, we need to do. I have a simple philosophy in this regard: the more people who come through our doors, the more people we have an opportunity to reach for Christ. I want us to be able to put up a plaque this year (and every year) that reads: IN THE YEAR 2003 SOMETHING HAPPENED HERE!

11.

One Mistake

I found myself thinking about him one Monday morning as his team, the Chicago White Sox, sought their first World Series' title since his days as their star. If he was not the greatest baseball player ever, I think it is safe to say that there have not been five major leaguers in the history of the game who were as good as he.

His lifetime batting average of .356 stands as the third best of all time. He set a record that will never be broken when he batted .408 during his rookie season in the majors as a member of the Cleveland Indians.

Babe Ruth said of him, "I copied (his) style because I thought he was the greatest hitter I had ever seen…He's the guy who made me a hitter."

An outstanding pitcher of that era, Ernie Shore, said, "Everything he hit was really blessed. He could break bones with his shots. Blindfold me and I could still tell you when (he) hit the ball. It had a special crack."

In May of 2002, his famous bat, Black Betsy, was bought by a collector from Pennsylvania for the outlandish sum of $577,610, purportedly the highest price ever paid for a bat. He was not just a hitter. He was unerring in the field as well, with a powerful and accurate throwing arm. He ran the bases with savvy, stealing as many as thirty-four bases in a season.

But in spite of all of his accomplishments, he never made it to the Hall of Fame, and he died in relative obscurity in his native South Carolina in 1951.

His name was "Shoeless" Joe Jackson, and he made only one mistake in his major league career. Prior to the

1919 World Series against the Cincinnati Reds, Jackson accepted a bribe of $5,000 to help throw the series. Though he later claimed that he had not cheated (he batted .375 in the series) and that he twice tried to give the money back, he was banished from baseball by commissioner Kennesaw Mountain Landis in 1920, along with seven teammates.

It is a scary thought that one mistake could ruin a baseball player's career, but what is scarier is that one mistake could destroy a Christian's reputation and witness. You play the game well, but let your guard down for a moment, and the end result is failure. Paul wisely reminds us in I Corinthians 10:12, "If you think you are standing firm, be careful that you don't fall!"

12.

Dr. Strangeglove

They played him at first base because, as any baseball player knows, it is the one place you can put a lousy fielder and hope to minimize the damage he does. I guess they had tried him everywhere else and come to the conclusion that hand-eye coordination was not a part of his genetic makeup.

Even so, at first base he would earn the nickname of "Dr. Strangeglove." Grounders would go between his legs, pop-ups would sometimes almost hit him in the head, throws from infielders would be muffed if they were off-line or in the dirt. He stills holds the major league record for the most errors in one season by a first baseman: twenty-nine.

He certainly wasn't fast or much of a base runner either. In his ten-year major league career, he stole a total of two bases. That's right, two stolen bases in over 1100 games! If you needed a pinch runner, you might as well forget about Stu—he was far too uncoordinated to be cunning on the base path. He couldn't hit for average either. He had a tendency to strikeout way too often and had a career batting average of only .264.

But the Pittsburgh Pirates played him anyway! The reason? Dick Stuart knew how to hit home runs. One year in the minor leagues, at Lincoln, Nebraska, Stuart had sixty-six homers. Every time he came to the plate, there was the distinct possibility that he just might hit a ball out of the park. And that one talent was enough to keep Dr. Strangeglove in the major leagues for a decade.

Sometimes in the church, there are those of us who are intimidated by the multi-talented stars who seem to be able to do anything and everything. Such versatile people, I will admit, are a great blessing to the kingdom of God, especially when they have willing hearts.

But I think we have a greater need today for some Dr. Strangegloves. We need some one-talented people who may not do a lot of things well, but are very good in one particular area of life. Search your heart. Is there some ability God has given you that you can give back to Him in service? Why not take your gift off of the shelf and get in the game!

13.

Prospects, Suspects and Others

It was a file I had kept through the years of ministry, but misplaced in our move to Grayson. It had special significance to me, and sometimes when I was very discouraged about the Lord's work in the local church, I would take it out and look at it.

It contained numerous 4" X 6" cards which we had used in our evangelistic calling program at Ironton. "Prospect cards" we called them. That was really a misnomer—they were actually "suspect cards." Most of the names on the cards were those of people who were not really good prospects for membership, but who were on the periphery. Maybe they have visited the church at one time. Maybe they had relatives who were members. Perhaps I had helped them deal with a family crisis. Regardless, they were close enough to warrant a personal visit from time to time.

After each visit, the calling team would list the response of the individual to the call. Each card allowed information for four or five personal calls. Then, we would staple a second card to first and start over again. There would be four or five more calls, then another new card stapled on. Some of the cards in the file had a half a dozen cards stapled to them, meaning that twenty or even thirty calls had been made on the particular person over the years!

Each card set in the file told a story about the individual whose name was on the front. For instance, we had first called on Joe back in February of 1977, and he had told us at that time that he would soon make a decision for Christ. Four stapled cards and twenty calls later, Joe was still saying the same thing in 1985. But there, in bold red letters on the front of the first card, was the word "Baptism"—March 3, 1986!

There was Sue who had received visits eleven times, and eleven times had said "no" to the invitation as an immersed believer to become a member of the Central congregation. Then, the red letters on the front of the card, "Transfer of Membership"—June 7, 1983!

Then there was Bill who refused to let us in his house the first time we went to visit him, according to his card. A dozen calls and a Jules Miller film series later, he and his wife made their confession of faith and were baptized into Christ.

I kept this file to remind me that it takes time for some folks to make up their minds about Jesus and His place in their lives. Now, I agree with you that it shouldn't be that way.

In the first century world, many people accepted Christ after hearing their first sermon. It generally doesn't happen so quickly in modern-day America.

But we who love the Lord and these precious people don't give up. We keep calling, preaching, encouraging, challenging; patiently doing whatever we must to point them to life eternal. Eleventh hour conversions are just as valid as those that occur during the first hour (Matthew 20:8-20).

14.

Check!

While on vacation recently, we went to church on Sunday, arriving just before the service started. We slipped into a pew near the back because the building was nearly full. Seated in front of us was a middle-aged woman with two little boys. Probably their grandmother, it was obvious that she had her hands full trying to keep them under control.

The younger boy was about five years old, redheaded and full of life. The grandmother was working hard to keep his shenanigans to a minimum, but she might as well have been trying to nail Jell-O to the wall! Finally, she yanked him up and left, no doubt to apply the rod of correction.

My attention shifted to the older boy who was perhaps eight or nine years of age. He had been sitting quietly during most of the service, pencil in hand, marking something down in the church bulletin. On closer inspection, I noticed what it was. On the "Service of Worship" page, he was carefully marking a check by each part of the service schedule as it was completed. Prelude—check; opening prayer—check; first hymn—check; second hymn—check; offering—check!

I couldn't help but be amused. To this little boy, a worship service evidently was a lot like a trip to the dentist—something to be endured. He had found a way to make it more bearable, passing the time checking off the components of the service, anxiously waiting for the opportunity to check off the benediction!

I was able to refocus my thinking in time to hear a pretty good sermon by a preacher who was preaching for the third time that morning, but afterwards thoughts of the little boy lingered. I found myself wondering if this is the way a lot of adults, as well, look at worship. Is it a blessed privilege or simply a necessary duty to be endured? Do we say with the Psalmist, "I rejoiced with those who said to me, Let us go to the house of the Lord" (Psalm 122:1)? Or are we, mentally at least, checking off the list?

15.

The Danger of Isolation

I was awakened early one morning by the thoughts of something I had seen on the Discovery Channel late the night before. I am not usually affected by such presentations, but the horror of this particular story jolted me out of my slumber and kept me from being able to fall asleep again.

It was video taken somewhere in Africa, I assume. A baby elephant was separated somehow from his mother. He was left to wander about, trying to find her or at least some herd of elephants that might take him in. Being so young, he had to have a mother's milk to survive. He could not simply drink water and eat the foliage, which is the diet of older elephants.

He found a herd of bull elephants, but they wanted nothing to do with his attempts to become a part of their group. They pushed him with their trunks and kicked him with their feet. He wandered off after his repeated efforts to join the group failed.

He then found a maternal herd with their young. Sometimes they will adopt an orphan and allow him to suckle, but not this time. The old, lead mother elephant actually tried to kill the baby by goring him violently.

Disoriented, weak, and lonely, our little friend wandered off into the night. And then it happened. A hungry group of hyenas sensed his plight and surrounded him. Although there were several bull elephants nearby, they did nothing— nothing but watch as the hyenas attacked our poor, defenseless victim and literally ate him alive. I am usually not so emotional, but the scene almost reduced me to tears. How I hurt for the little guy!

The sad story reinforces an important truth. A baby elephant need fear no enemy, not even the king of jungle, when he is with his herd. But let him become separated and he becomes an easy prey for most of the predators of the wild.

The application to the Christian life is obvious. There is no such thing as solitary Christianity. We need each other. A large part of our spiritual sustenance comes from the rich fellowship we enjoy as we worship and serve together.

To separate ourselves from the church, deliberately or unintentionally, results in making us extremely vulnerable to Satan's attacks. He's no simple hyena, however. The Bible tells us that he prowls around like a roaring lion looking for someone to devour (I Peter 5:8). Stay close to your Christian brothers and sisters. It is the only safe way to travel through this world!

16.

DiMaggio and the Umpire

It is one of those apocryphal stories that we preachers love to tell. Supposedly, it is the only time that Joe DiMaggio ever said anything to the home plate umpire after an at bat. The Yankee Clipper was a perfect gentleman, both on and off the field. In his years as a player, he was never one to respond verbally or otherwise to bad calls, even when they seemed obvious.

But one day, after taking a called third strike, he turned to the umpire and said something and then walked away.

After the game, the sport writers went looking for the umpire because what DiMaggio had done was so uncharacteristic.

"What did he say? What did he say?" was the query of all of the newsmen of the man calling balls and strikes behind the plate.

The umpire's reply was not what they expected. He quoted the Yankee centerfielder as saying, "I wish I had that pitch over again." Evidently it was a good pitch, one that "Joltin' Joe" could probably have driven out of the ballpark if he had swung. But he didn't, and he went back to the dugout lamenting the fact that he had failed to act when he could have and should have.

Some of us probably have a similar feeling as we look back on the past year. We stood at the plate and looked at some balls that we should have swung at. Instead of acting in a timely manner, we procrastinated. Sometimes we were guilty of staying in the dugout and not even coming to the plate. Too often, the box score after the day's game had nothing but a series of goose eggs after our names.

What can we do about it? Perhaps we can learn from DiMaggio. We can accept and admit our failures, but go back to the dugout and get ready for our next at bat.

There will be another pitch and another opportunity to knock the ball out of the park—as long as we stay in the game. That's the crucial part, staying in the game. The apostle Paul said it this way, "But this one thing I do: forgetting what is behind and straining toward what is ahead, I press on toward the goal to win the prize" (Philippians 3:13, 14).

17.

Send Up Lumber

A good friend told me the story from his days as a funeral director in southern Ohio. An old African American preacher was officiating at the funeral of a church member who had never really gotten involved in the work of the kingdom. The preacher proceeded to plow close to the corn as we would say back home, not pulling any punches about the deceased sister's life.

"When Sister Jones got to heaven, St. Peter walked with her down the streets of gold toward her new home. She noticed the huge mansions on each side of the street. They were beautiful and lavish in their accessories.

"Sister Jones began to think in great excitement of her own mansion to which St. Peter was leading her. How wonderful it was going to be!

"They arrived at the proper address, but there was no mansion. Sitting on the lot was a tiny little cottage with barely enough room for even one person. Drab and plain, it was enough to make Sister Jones want to cry.

"'St. Peter,' she exclaimed. 'I don't understand. Here we have passed dozens of beautiful mansions and my house is nothing but a tiny little shoebox by comparison. Why don't I have a mansion like everyone else?"

"'Sister,' St. Peter replied solemnly, 'To have a mansion, you've got to send up lumbah. You didn't send up any lumbah.'"

Although it should not be our primary goal, we are all "sending up lumber" for our heavenly mansion with the work we do for God's kingdom here. Remember Jesus' admonition from the Sermon on the Mount, "Lay up treasures for yourself in heaven" (Matthew 6:20)?

One of the reasons we are emphasizing the involvement of all of our members in the Lord's work here at First Church is because we want every member's eternal accommodations to be glorious and wonderful.

To use the words of the old preacher, we have too many brothers and sisters at First Church who aren't sending up much lumbah! The remedy is for all of us to find our place of service. Remember, we are all building for eternity!

18.

A President's Bible

Congress once issued a special edition of Thomas Jefferson's Bible. It was simply a copy of our Bible with all references to the supernatural eliminated. Jefferson, in making his selections from the scriptures, confined himself solely to moral teachings of Jesus. The closing words of the Jeffersonian version are these: "There laid they Jesus, and rolled a great stone to the mouth of the sepulcher and departed."

What a tragic story the life of Jesus would be if Jefferson was right. What a different world we would be living in today! You see, most of the beauty and much of the wonder of the twenty-first century world can be traced to the efforts of those who know the tomb was empty and that Jesus was alive again.

Go ahead. Remove all of the blessings of mankind motivated by a belief in the resurrected Lord and see what you have left! Subtract the wonderful works of the literary world and the priceless art that originated in the hearts of those who believed.

Take away the compassionate and benevolent efforts through the centuries done by those who followed a resurrected Lord. Discard the clinics, sanitariums, hospitals, and mission stations built in honor to His name. Rid the world of the disaster relief organizations that ultimately trace their start to a belief that Jesus is alive.

What would you have left if Jefferson was right? What kind of world would we be living in today? A world devoid of most of its beauty and all of its hope!

Thomas Jefferson was a brilliant man, but he was wrong. The burial of Jesus was not the final chapter in the story of this Galilean carpenter. Read on, my friends, and see. On the third day after Calvary, the tomb was empty. Jesus was alive again! He had burst the bands of death and conquered the grave. That is the real Good News for us today.

19.

Life in a Jar

The two half-gallon jars I used in yesterday's sermon are setting on my desk this morning.[4] As I look at them, I find myself thinking once more of the lesson they teach about ordering our priorities.

The first jar is filled to the brim with big rocks only. You could not get any more big rocks into it at all. But, as I pointed out in the message, it is not really full.

The second jar contains big rocks to its brim, but also has gravel that I put into the crevices. Then I put as much sand as I could into the jar, filling in the small pockets left empty by the gravel. Finally I poured water into the jar and watched as it filled the remaining space left by the sand.

The point of the illustration? Some eager beaver would respond, "The point is, no matter how full your schedule, if you really try hard, you can always fit some things into it."

No! As I indicated in the sermon, "<u>The point is, if you don't put the big rocks in first, you'll never get them in at all</u>!"

The big rocks represent the really important priorities of our lives: time for God, time for family, and time for others.

Too often our time schedules dictate to us instead of vice versa. The gravel, sand, and water responsibilities are so present and numerous that we find ourselves giving undue attention to them. We fill our jars with this minutia and then find that there is no room for the big rocks. There is no time left for the really important things of life.

My suggestion? Let's empty the jar and start over! Starting today, let's put the big rocks in first. Take time for God. May we make our quiet time with Him a central part of our daily routine. May we meditate upon His Word and listen to His voice as He speaks to us through His Spirit. Let us also reestablish the Lord's Day as the Lord's Day in our lives.

Then, we need to carve out a place for our families in our daily schedules. Realizing that quality time is impossible without the proper quantity of time, let's work to build a place for our spouse and children in our daily calendars.

Finally, we must make room for our fellowman. We need to follow the pattern of our Lord Who, though He carried the weight of the world on His shoulders, still found time for people. Let us allow our schedules to be interrupted by others in need.

It is a simple concept, but I really believe that it embodies the truth about the use of our time and energy. If we make room for the big rocks, we will be amazed at how much space is left for the gravel, sand, and water! God will bless our "leftover" time in ways we cannot imagine, if we are willing to get our priorities straight and put first things first.

PART VII — PEOPLE

For many years, the *Reader's Digest* had a feature called "My Most Unforgettable Character." It was always my favorite part of the monthly magazine because it helped to reinforce the idea that the deeds of the rich and famous are often eclipsed by the actions of common ordinary folks.

It has been my good fortune to work with many such people during my lifetime of preaching and teaching. The most outstanding of these people do not fit into any particular category as to age, race, position, or gender. I have been amazed by a number of the very young, just beginning their life experience. I have been equally impacted by some who were in the twilight years of their earthly sojourn. I have learned from both men and women whose lives were exceptional in some sense. I have been inspired by both the culturally and economically diverse.

All of these people have been my teachers, most of them without realizing it. They would not think of themselves as heroes or heroines, but they have certainly served that role in my personal life. As they have inspired me to live better and work harder for God and good, I offer their stories to you, hoping that you will be equally challenged in a positive direction.

1.

The Influence of a Life and a Death

It was a beautiful fall day in mid-October on the campus of Kentucky Christian College. The late afternoon sun was streaming brilliant rays of light, buoying the spirits of those of us who had gathered for intramural sports. I was helping to officiate the flag-football game. In an early series of downs, the quarterback of the offensive team faded back and threw a deep pass that sailed over the outstretched arms of the fastest player on the field, Greg Bailey.

Greg came jogging back towards the scrimmage line when he suddenly fell to the ground. I thought he had tripped on something, but I noticed that his body was arched in a rigid position and that his single breath was followed by one large exhalation that raised the dust beneath his nostrils.

Frozen by the scene, I stood by, while a couple of fellow players rolled Greg over and tried to help him breathe. One young man began to do CPR while others rushed to call an ambulance. The college president pulled up in his automobile and got out, staring at the scene in disbelief. The heroic rescue efforts failed. Greg Bailey was dead.

Twenty-one years old, an honor student with a weekend preaching ministry, Greg had been discharged from the service a couple of years before because of a heart murmur. Sobered by his condition, he had wasted no time in entering Bible college and working to prepare himself to share God's Good News. With absolutely no exaggeration, I can tell you he was the most dedicated young man I ever met in my four years of study at KCC.

And now it was over. Or was it? The lives that Greg would affect with his short life and, seemingly, untimely death are too numerous to count. Scores of young preacher boys on that campus would henceforth preach with even greater conviction, knowing indeed that the messenger is simply "a dying man speaking to dying men." I count myself among that number.

I have no doubt that if God had chosen to let Greg live, he would have influenced many lives for Christ. But I also have no doubt, that in his death, his long term impact on the kingdom of God was even greater. Many of us questioned God's decision on that day, but most of us quit questioning a long time ago as we saw the ongoing effect of Greg's death on those of us who remained. God is sovereign and He can be trusted. Greg got an early pass to glory and the rest of us were encouraged to become even better soldiers of the cross.

2.

Pursued by the Hound of Heaven

I guess if I was attempting to summarize Paul's life, I would have to say that he had spent it trying to run from God. A man of quick wit and abundant energy, he had busied himself with his job and large farm. Unschooled, but a deep thinker, he said he was an agnostic, but could never quite convince me that it was true.

Friends of members of the church where I was preaching at the time, he and his wife would attend our services frequently. I began making visits to their home, telling them about Jesus. Norma responded readily to the claims of the gospel and was baptized into Christ within a few short weeks.

But Paul had far too many questions about the validity of Christianity to be so easily swayed. He laughed at my attempts at persuasion and tried to punch holes in my arguments that Jesus was the only way. I would have given up on him, but there was something about Paul that convinced me that, deep within, God was dealing with him.

Like Francis Thompson in his classic Christian poem, "The Hound of Heaven," it seemed to me that he was trying to flee a God who would not let him go.

I fled Him, down the nights and down the days;

I fled Him, down the arches of the years;

I fled Him, down the labyrinthine ways of my own mind.[5]

Then the midnight of Paul's soul came. Stricken with a disease that would eventually take his life, his thoughts became deeper and more somber. He began to understand Thompson's words placed in the mouth of God:

All which I took from thee I did but take,

Not for thy harms,

But just that thou might'st seek it in My arms.[6]

And, miracle of miracles, one night as the invitation hymn was sung, Paul stepped forward to give his life to Christ.

I think of Paul from time to time when the work seems hard and fruitless and when people seem to be totally resistant to the Good News. When should we give up on the lost? Not until God does, my friend. Then and only then.

3.

Life Begins at Eighty

It was one of those once-in-a-lifetime events for a preacher. The taxi pulled up to the verandah of our back door at Central Christian Church in Ironton, Ohio. Very gingerly stepping out of the rear seat was an elderly man who walked with a limp and a cane.

It was just about time for church services to begin on a Sunday morning, and the man asked for the pastor. They found me, probably hiding in my office, as I often did before preaching, to pray and collect my thoughts.

"Oh, no," I said to myself, "Another benevolent need." It is a common practice for people to wait until Sunday morning to confess dire circumstances, hoping to get a quick resolution from sympathetic churchgoers.

But Otto Bragg was different. With a laugh and grin, he said to me, "I have come to be baptized."

Although I had never talked with the man before, it soon became apparent that was what he wanted! A resident of one of our local nursing homes, he had attended our annual nursing home luncheon a few days before and was impressed with the kindness and love expressed by our church family.

Mr. Bragg had moved back to Ironton after over fifty years spent in San Francisco. He had no immediate family, except for a couple of nieces who lived some distance away.

"I want to be a member of this church. I want to be baptized," he said. I hurriedly discussed the matter with him and confirmed that his request was for real. In his old age, he had decided he needed spiritual roots, and so he had called a taxi and presented himself to obey the Gospel.

He sat through the service and came forward at the invitation. Some of our men helped him upstairs to our baptistry. In his feeble condition, it was not the easiest baptism I have ever performed, but it was certainly one of the most memorable.

His parting words as one of our families prepared to drive him back to the nursing home were classic, "Preacher, they say life begins at forty. They're wrong. Life begins at eighty!"

And, of course, he was right. At the age of eighty, Otto Bragg had become a child of the King. True life was his for the first time and he knew it!

As I look back at his conversion, there are two thoughts in my mind. First of all, how fortunate he was to still have a tender heart and the opportunity to be saved at his age. And, secondly, how sad to waste eighty years living without Jesus!

4.

A Heart that Is Finally Whole

Seth Hill went to sleep at his home in Wadsworth, Ohio, last Wednesday night and woke up on Thursday morning in heaven. His enlarged and scarred heart began racing at 6 a.m., and his pacemaker simply couldn't keep up. Seth was only twenty-five years old.

Many of you here at First Church in Grayson remember him from the summer of 2001 when he served as our Children's Ministry intern. He did an exceptional job, which didn't surprise any of us who knew him. He did so well in his two required Sunday evening preaching stints that we asked him to preach on the Sunday morning he completed his internship.

Seth had just begun his work this summer as Student Minister of the Northwest Christian Church in Tallmadge, OH. Teresa, Megan, Jenny Leamon and I traveled there yesterday to attend the memorial service and to celebrate the life of this special young man.

The lessons he taught us during his brief, but brilliant, sojourn in this world will not be forgotten by those of us who came to love him.

His quiet courage in the face of daunting physical problems stands out as perhaps the most striking lesson. With a heart problem that had plagued him most of his life, Seth Hill lived with the constant knowledge that any day could be his last day on earth. Rather than allowing this fact to move him to a life of self-pitying inactivity, Seth made his health problems an even greater reason to get busy now in serving the Jesus he loved.

Some of us spend an entire lifetime trying to make an impact for God and good in this world. Seth did it in a few short years with a style and passion that were uniquely his own. He will be missed, but his labors will continue to bear fruit for years to come if our Lord tarries. Earth's loss is heaven's gain, and I am comforted by the knowledge that there are absolutely no heart problems or defects in that celestial city. Well done, my dear young brother, well done!

5.

A Question from Stephanie

Sometimes when you are teaching, you will be asked a question that really gives you pause. Such was the case just a few nights ago in my General Psychology class at Ohio University Southern.

I have a large group this quarter, over forty students in all. Some are just out of high school and starting their college experience; some have been away from the academic environment for a decade or longer; and some are precocious high-schoolers who are getting a head start on their higher education goals.

It was a little girl in that last group who raised her hand and asked a question I had never pondered. Perhaps I need to tell you that we were discussing motivated behavior and were focusing in on the subject of "thirst." I had made the statement that we get thirsty two ways: either by the ingestion of too much salt or the depletion of body fluids.

I went on to explain that any way the body loses fluids (perspiration, urination, regurgitation) tends to create a signal that tells our brain we are thirsty. Stephanie's question was not an attempt to be funny or flippant. She was obviously very serious when she asked, "If you cry a lot of tears, does it make you thirsty?"

My answer to the question is not nearly as important as the fact that Stephanie asked it, in my estimation. One time I remember someone say, "If you listen closely enough, you can hear when a heart is breaking."

In Stephanie's words I sensed not a broken heart, but the plea of a young lady who probably wanted me to know that sorrow has been a part of her young life. It was as though she was testing me to see if I was really listening—and really cared. We had a conversation after class that I hope helped her see that counseling and encouragement are available if she needs them.

I must confess that I am not always as attentive in such situations as I need to be. Sometimes people are crying out and my ears are closed to their problems. Forgive me, Lord, for my self-absorption and my lack of concern for others. Please open my ears and my heart so I can be an instrument of your peace today.

6.

The Cost of Following Jesus

Among the slides from my 1989 trip to India, I have one that is very special to me. It shows a young Indian man standing in front of the little church building where he preaches. His name is Mohammed Philip, and he and I have more in common that just our names. We are brothers in the Lord and fellow ministers of the gospel. I have kept his picture to remind me of the price some people are willing to pay in order to follow Jesus.

Mohammed Philip grew up as a Muslim in his native Kerala. India has a population of over one billion people, with about 150 million Muslims and over 800 million Hindus. Although Kerala state is the most Christian in the entire country, the percentage of those who follow Jesus is miniscule by comparison to the other two religions that dominate.

I don't know exactly how he came to know Jesus. I imagine it was through the work of P. V. Alexander and his colleagues, probably through the efforts of the Kerala Christian Bible College. Regardless, in the mind of many of his countrymen, this young man with a wife and little child did the unthinkable; he turned his back on Islam and embraced Christianity.

Almost immediately, his wife deserted him, taking their child and returning to her parents' home in the hills of northern Kerala. To the followers of the prophet Mohammed, there is nothing worse than becoming a Christian. It was much safer, from a worldly perspective, for her to leave him and go back to her childhood home.

But Mohammed Philip loved his wife and desperately missed his child. He journeyed to her parents' home to plead with her to return. Her father and brothers greeted him at the door and beat him severely, almost killing him. Bruised and broken-hearted, he returned to southern Kerala and prepared for the ministry. He had found the pearl of great price and nothing, absolutely nothing, would keep him from sharing it with others.

What does it cost to follow Jesus? The truth is, in some parts of the world, the price is much higher than it is in America. But at any price, it is worth it. If you don't believe me, just ask Mohammed Philip.

7.

Misadventures in the Smithsonian

A number of years ago my good friend, Lester Bryant, and I took Washington, DC, by storm and almost ended up in some major trouble. Although he has since gone to be with the Lord, I find myself sometimes thinking of our adventure in the nation's capitol.

Through the generosity of a church member, we had received tickets to the inauguration of Ronald Reagan, complete with train fare and hotel accommodations in Alexandria, Virginia. Monday was the day before the actual ceremony and the weather was beautiful! The temperature was in the mid-sixties, and Lester and I decided to do some sightseeing downtown.

I wanted to see some of the exhibits at the nearby National Museum of American History, part of the Smithsonian Institution, located on the Mall. We saw a line of people going in, dressed in suits and trench coats. We just happened to be in suits and trench coats, too (Hey, it was the inaugural week in Washington. What did you think I would have on, jeans?). So Lester and I just got in line and followed them in.

We wandered upstairs to some of the exhibits from the colonial period of America, and I was amazed to discover that we had the place to ourselves! There was no one at the museum that day! I just assumed everyone was preoccupied with the festivities and that Lester and I were the only people in Washington who were interested in American history. Boy, were we having fun!

But suddenly, our visit was over. A security guard arrived and asked us who we were and what we were doing in the building. It seems there was a private reception for Vice-President Elect Bush at the museum that afternoon, and the building was closed to the public.

Soon another security guard arrived, and Lester and I were very unceremoniously escorted downstairs via an elevator, being questioned along the way. They couldn't figure how we got in. Evidently, suits and trench coats were the secret service uniform for the day, and we were just lucky enough to look the part.

I think the only thing that saved us was the obvious fact that we were hayseeds from southeastern Ohio who didn't have a clue as to what was going on. Hey, you might be laughing at me, but how many of you ever had a private afternoon at the Smithsonian? Ah, America, it's a great country, isn't it?

8.

Like Father, Like Son

It is a truism that has stood the test of time, "Like father, like son." We saw it played out once again in the life of John Mark Pemberton, who unexpectedly went home to be with the Lord last Monday afternoon. Somewhere over the skies between Portland and Cincinnati on a return flight from a speaking engagement for Second Mile International, this brave soldier of the cross breathed his last breath.

I had often remarked of John Mark's father, John Pemberton, that he was the oldest man I had ever known. I meant no disrespect. I was only saying that this mission pioneer had worn his body out serving Christ alongside his equally dedicated wife, Marjorie, in southern Africa. John Pemberton knew of only one way to serve the Lord, and that was with all of his heart, his soul and his being. In the end it probably, from a worldly perspective, carved a dozen years off of his earthly sojourn.

And so it would be with John Mark. Assuming the helm of the mission a little over a decade ago, he would accept the mantle of responsibility with the same zeal and determination that had marked the ministry of his parents. The stresses of the work in Zimbabwe have been great, especially with the AIDS pandemic in sub-Saharan Africa and the instability of the oppressive Mugabe regime.

Six years ago, when I visited the mission, the American dollar was the equivalent of 54 Zim dollars. Today, the exchange rate is 62,000 to 1 and going higher by the minute. Trying to raise enough money to keep the mission afloat in such inflationary times was a behemoth task that I believe literally wore John Mark's heart out. His last words to his mother from the Portland airport as he awaited his flight were, "Mom, I am so tired."

Thus, much too soon for those of us who loved him and appreciated his work, our brother has been called to his rest. Our thoughts and prayers are with his dear wife and co-laborer, Leanna, their three daughters and precious granddaughter.

9.

On Any Street Anywhere

It wasn't any voyeuristic tendency, really, that led me to drive to the Sedgwick Meadows subdivision of Ironton, Ohio, last Friday before my psychology class at Ohio University Southern. It was just the fact that we lived for twelve years at 1752 Phillip Street, and I couldn't believe what the news media were saying had happened at 1740 Phillip Street a few weeks before.

Sedgwick Meadows is a stereotypical small-town subdivision with neat houses and well-manicured lawns. When we were residents, our girls played up and down the block with their neighborhood friends. Some of the finest people I know in the world live there.

I slowed the car at the 1740 address and noted how much the house looked like any other house on Phillip Street. The shrubbery and flowers in the front yard were tastefully placed and made the home just as attractive from the outside as any other on the block.

But in the middle of the front yard were numerous bouquets of flowers, toys, a guardian angel, a cheerleader doll dressed in the black and orange of the Fighting Tigers—an obvious memorial. The yellow police tape surrounding the yard added evidence that this was no ordinary home on a quiet small-town street.

It was here that a little girl named Seleana lived and died this past summer. It was in this backyard that her lifeless body was found buried in a thirty gallon trash can, four feet below the surface where she'd played.

Her pictures in the local media indicate that she was a beautiful eight year-old with a winning smile and her whole life before her. But someone thought differently. Her mother and step-father have disappeared and are charged with her murder.

My eyes became unfocused as I looked at the scene and thought of a world where such a thing could happen. I was reminded once again that the battle of good and evil rages not only on godless distant shores, but also right in our own backyards.

Up and down your street and mine are people who desperately need to know about Jesus Christ and God's love. Not only for themselves, but also for their families. Sure, we need to send missionaries to India and Africa and South America, but maybe we ought to start our outreach efforts with the family down the road or the new couple in the next block. Their need for Christ may be more pressing than we realize.

END NOTES

Part I

1. "nuclear family." *Merriam-Webster Online Dictionary.* 2008. http://www.merriam-webster.com (3 August 2009).

Part IV

2. Reprinted by permission of the publishers and the Trustees of Amherst College from *The Poems of Emily Dickinson,* Thomas H. Johnson, ed., Cambridge, Mass: The Belknap Press of Harvard University Press, Copyright 1951, 1955, 1979, 1983 by the President and Fellows of Harvard College.

3. Cook, Roy. *One Hundred and One Famous Poems* (New York: McGraw-Hill, 1984), 44.

Part VI

4. The "big rocks" illustration is usually attributed to Dr Stephen Covey who uses it in his seminars.

Part VII

5. Thompson, Francis. *The Hound of Heaven* (Harrisburg, PA: Morehouse Publishing, 1982), 4.

6. Ibid.